BOWLING

D0221604

About the Authors

Charlene Agne-Traub has taught bowling in five states over the past twenty-nine years and has coached both men's and women's teams at the collegiate level. One of her bowlers won the Illinois-Indiana collegiate regional singles competition and bowled at the WIBC tournament in Las Vegas. An avid bowler, she currently partic-ipates in two leagues and local and state tournaments. She carries an average in the mid-170s. She competed in the open division of the WIBC national tournaments in St. Louis in 1982 and Lansing, Michigan, in 1992, and Reno, Nevada in 1997. Her doubles team placed ninth in St. Louis and fiftieth in Lansing, averaging 189 for the nine tournament games. She is a member of the National, Virginia, and Washington, D.C., 600 clubs and a past member of the Virginia Bowling Queens. Charlene is a certified health education specialist with bachelor's and master's degrees in physical education and a doctoral degree in health education. Most recently, she has taught bowling at Howard University in Washington, D.C. Her published work includes professional journal articles in the fields of health, physical education, and leisure studies and a book on the history of *volkssporting* in the United States. Charlene Agne-Traub has been solely responsible for revisions for the fifth, sixth, seventh, and eighth editions of this highly popular book on bowling.

Joan Martin taught bowling at the University of Wisconsin and at the University of California at Los Angeles for over twenty years. She has been a league bowler and has participated as a special lecturer, not only in various bowling clinics sponsored by Lifetime Sports, but also in many school clinics in the Los Angeles area. Besides having been a successful coach of this universally popular activity, she has con-tributed to the literature in the *Research Quarterly* of the American Alliance of Health, Physical Education, Recreation, and Dance and the *Journal of Sports Medicine.* Joan Martin was the original author of this book.

Ruth Tandy first taught bowling in an antiquated facility with "grooved" lanes and no pinsetters. Since then she has taught bowling at the Ohio State University lanes and at the Texas Woman's University where she coached the bowling team. She teaches at both the undergraduate and graduate levels and specialized in the sociology of sport. She has published several sport psychology and sport sociology articles in professional journals. She was active in the National Association for Girls and Women in Sports and in sports officiating and has served on the national rules committees of several sport activities.

Bowling

Eighth Edition

Charlene Agne-Traub
Burke, Virginia

Joan L. Martin
Los Angeles, California

Ruth E. Tandy
Denton, Texas

Boston, Massachusetts   Burr Ridge, Illinois
Dubuque, Iowa   Madison, Wisconsin   New York, New York
San Francisco, California   St. Louis, Missouri

WCB/McGraw-Hill

A Division of The **McGraw·Hill** *Companies*

BOWLING: EIGHTH EDITION

This book is printed on recycled, acid-free paper containing 10% postconsumer waste.

8 9 0   DOC/DOC   0 9 8 7 6

ISBN-13: 978-0-697-34539-4

ISBN-10: 0-697-34539-4

Publisher: *Ed Bartell*
Sponsoring editor: *Vicki Malinee*
Marketing manager: *Pamela S. Cooper*
Project manager: *Ann Morgan*
Production supervisor: *Deb Donner*
Designer: *K. Wayne Harms*
Cover designer: © *Steven Marks/Image Bank*
Art editor: *Joyce Watters*
Compositor: *Shepherd, Inc.*
Typeface: *10/12 Times Roman*
Printer: *R. R. Donnelley & Sons Company*

Library of Congress Card Catalog Number: 97–14665

Agne-Traub, Charlene E.
   Bowling/Charlene Agne-Traub, Joan L. Martin, Ruth E. Tandy.—
8th ed.
      p. cm.
   Martin's name appears first on previous editions.
   Includes bibliographical references (p.) and index.
   ISBN 0–697–34539–4
   1. Bowling.   I. Martin, Joan L.   II. Tandy, Ruth E.   III. Title.
GV903.M35 1997
794.6—dc21   97–14665 CIP

http://www.mhhe.com

Contents

Preface

The eighth edition provides up-to-date and expanded information on the sport of bowling. Some new photos either replace previous ones or are added in an effort to illustrate the text material. Information was reorganized where appropriate; for example, historical information once presented in the league bowling chapter is now part of the first chapter on bowling history. Additional information on bowling for the disabled and on bowling equipment is provided. The language of bowling chapter is now located at the end of the text to make it easier to find and refer to terms. The rules section is completely revamped and expanded. The entire text, including references, is updated to provide the most current information. The book will serve the needs of beginners and seasoned bowlers in instructional, recreational, or league environments.

Bowling is one of the leading participatory sports for Americans of all ages: children, teenagers, college students, family groups, and senior citizens. This book is designed to assist all eager enthusiasts in learning the basic skills that lead to optimum bowling performance and pleasure.

There is no substitute for good instruction, but good instruction also profits from reinforcement by the written word and by visual cues. Most people seek and appreciate opportunities to find out more about what they are attempting to learn or do. They require an explanation of the "why" and the "when," as well as the "how to."

The material presented delves into all aspects of the game including history, popularity, basic and advanced techniques, official rules and scoring, etiquette, bowling language, equipment, and facilities. Both the novice and the experienced bowler will discover many helpful hints to assist them in correcting faults in their approach or delivery and adjusting to differences in lane conditions, with some thoughts on strategies and points of concentration for competitive bowling. The sequencing of chapters is not meant to be a concrete format; rather, flexibility allows the reader to pick and choose the order of interest.

Self-evaluation and competency-based questions are distributed throughout this book. These afford the reader typical examples of the kinds of understanding and levels of skill that should be acquired as progress is made toward proficiency in bowling. The player should not only answer the printed questions but should pose additional ones as a self-check on learning. In some instances, you may find that you cannot respond fully and accurately to a question until you have read more extensively or have gained more playing experience. From time to time, you should return to troublesome questions until you are sure of the answers or have developed the necessary skills.

Many generous friends, colleagues, and students assisted in the preparation of the manuscript, photographs, and illustrations. The late Ruth Abernathy assisted with the first edition along with Jeff Must, Peggy Iden, Ann Stutts, and Don Sawyer. Our appreciation was extended to Iris Kimura and Charlene Agne for assistance with the fourth edition. Charlene Agne-Traub solely revised the fifth, sixth, seventh, and eighth editions. We are also indebted to the American Bowling Congress, the Women's International Bowling Congress, American Machine and Foundry, Brunswick Corporation, the National Bowling Council, and the National Bowling Hall of Fame and Museum for supplying us with pertinent information and materials. The past curator, Mr. Bruce Pluckhahn, and the current curator, Mr. John Dalzell, of the Bowling Hall of Fame and Museum in St. Louis, Missouri, were especially helpful. Thanks to the Howard University bowling students of Dr. Agne-Traub for their cooperation with the sixth edition. The assistance of Gary Traub, husband of Dr. Agne-Traub and an excellent bowler as well, was essential in the preparation of the sixth, seventh, and eighth editions.

Charlene E. Agne-Traub
Joan Martin
Ruth E. Tandy

The Beginning of Bowling

1

The term *bowl* is thought to be derived from the Saxon *bolla* and the Danish *bolle,* both meaning, in the literal sense, "bubble." The word later referred to any round or spherical object. Some authorities trace the word to the Latin *bulla,* or round ball, and others prefer the French derivation *boule,* meaning "ball."

Throwing, pitching, or rolling objects at targets has for centuries fulfilled an innate urge in humans, and the earliest records of such activity used as a game were discovered by an English Egyptologist, Sir Flinders Petrie. While examining the contents of an Egyptian child's grave, the burial date placed at 3200 B.C., he discovered implements and objects for playing a game very similar to our tenpins of today (fig. 1.1).

In other studies by Dr. Malcolm Rogers, curator of the San Diego Museum, an ancient bowling game as performed by the Polynesians was found in which small elliptical balls and round, flat discs of stone about four inches in diameter were used. The game was called *Ula Maika* and consisted of bowling or rolling the stones a distance of sixty feet, the length of our bowling lanes today.

Bowling's place of origin in Europe appears to have been in what is now northern Italy, where as early as 50 B.C. the Helvetii played *Boccie,* a game similar to modern Italian bowling.

These ancient forms of bowling were outdoor activities resembling the game of lawn bowling. Lawn bowling takes place on a grassy area, known as a green, where a ball is rolled at other objects, usually another ball. Bowling at pins actually originated as a religious ceremony in the cloisters of cathedrals in Germany as early as the third or fourth centuries A.D. It was then the custom for the canons to test the faith of their parishioners by having them place their pins at one end of the cloister and from the opposite end throw a ball at the pins which represented the *Heide* or heathen. If a hit was scored, this meant the parishioner was leading a pure and clean life and would be able to slay the heathen; if they were unsuccessful at hitting the pins, the parishioner's aim could be improved by more faithful attendance at church services. Those who were successful were called *keglers* and were honored and toasted at a dinner given at the conclusion of the tests.

The game ceased to be a religious endeavor and developed into a sport when the canons became intrigued and began *kegling* with their cathedral students. The game changed to include as many pins as there were *keglers.*

The first indoor bowling lanes are believed to have originated in England where, because of bad weather conditions, bowling on the open green (lawn bowling) was difficult. During the Middle Ages, to ensure year round activity, the wealthy enthusiasts of the game constructed bowling annexes to their residences.

Figure 1.1
Early Egyptians bowling. (Courtesy of American Bowling Congress)

Early Beginnings

On the continent, bowling, or ninepins, soon became a universal pastime (fig. 1.2). In Germany, as few as three pins and as many as seventeen were used until Martin Luther established nine as the ideal number. Luther was an enthusiastic bowler and built a bowling lane for his family. The French had a game called *Carreau* which was played long before the reign of Charlemagne. The Dutch pins version resembled skittles but with taller and narrower pins, especially the middle pin which was higher than the rest and called the kingpin. Curling, another adaptation of the ancient game of bowls, was introduced into Scotland by the Flemish in the sixteenth century. Bowling on ice, curling, became very popular in countries with severe winters and is still played today in Scotland, Canada, and some northern states of the United States.

In America, the early Dutch settlers brought the game of ninepins to Manhattan Island in 1626. Three citizens leased a plot formerly used as a parade ground or marketplace; this area was located at what is now the foot of Broadway in New York City. They enclosed it for a bowling green, and the little park still bears its original name of Peppercorn. Farther south in Virginia, the English settlers introduced lawn bowling.

Washington Irving, in "Rip Van Winkle" (1819), made one of the earliest references to pin bowling when he mentioned the thunder of the ball colliding with pins.

Figure 1.2
Ninepin bowling in Europe. (Courtesy of National Bowling Hall of Fame and Museum)

The early game probably reached the height of its popularity in the 1840s in New York where bowling lanes were found on nearly every block on Broadway and in various parts of the Bowery. Most of the matches were rigged, and this led to the abolition of bowling in New York, Connecticut, and Massachusetts when a law in 1841 declared it a gambling game. By 1850, gamblers and swindlers had complete control of the game of ninepins. The game of ninepins, which had the pins set in a diamond formation, had been condemned by the Puritans two hundred years earlier because men were devoting time to playing that could have been better spent in work. However, neither condemnation nor legislation could abolish enthusiasm for the game. Thus, ninepins at that time had to be played on the sly. Many a bowler sat in the stocks or in prison for defying the law. An ingenious hero, noting that the long-standing law prohibited "bowling at nine pins," added a tenth pin and a triangle formation to replace the diamond shape in which the pins were previously arranged, which not only circumvented the law but improved the game, and its growth began. By 1875, the game became well enough established that a "National Bowling Association" was formed to revise the rules and standardize the equipment. Although great credit is due this early association, it failed to survive, and the American Amateur Bowling Union replaced it in 1890. It, too, disintegrated due to its limitations, giving way in 1895 to the American Bowling Congress (ABC), whose objective was to help promote and elevate the game. As a result of insight, purposeful planning, and principles this organization is today the largest sports membership organization in the world. During the 1990–1991 season, a total of 6.7 million bowlers were members of organized leagues. The ABC had over 2.9 million members, the Women's International Bowling Congress (WIBC) had more than 2.8 million members, and the Young American Bowling Alliance (YABA) had over 1.0 million members.

The Women's National Bowling Association (WNBA) was established on November 28, 1916 with some forty members. This organization defines the rules for women's tenpin bowling in America. Before that time, ladies generally did not frequent bowling alleys or they did so at the risk of their reputations. They were allowed to bowl only when the men were not using the alleys, or they bowled behind curtains where they could not be seen. The game, however, was appealing to females and became more so as their wearing apparel became less restrictive. By 1908, they had national tournament competition, and by 1917, the National Women's Tournament in St. Louis had over 100 participants. That same year, the women had their own international organization. After the WNBA's eighth annual tournament in 1925 (fig. 1.3), the name was changed to the Women's International Bowling Congress.

In 1941, the American Junior Bowling Congress (AJBC) was organized. Since 1982, the Young American Bowling Alliance (YABA) has been the youth organization that governs the competition and supervises the instruction of boys and girls. In 1943, the National Bowling Council (NBC) was formed to coordinate all phases of bowling in the World War II effort. Today, this organization serves as the national coordinator for the sport. The NBC acts as the marketing arm for bowling and is also a clearinghouse for informational material, competitive news, and instructional clinics. It was not until 1966 that the ABC began to promote competitive collegiate bowling in order to bridge the gap between junior and adult bowling. The national intercollegiate tournament is sponsored by the Association of College Unions International.

Of what significance were the following sites in the history of bowling: an Egyptian child's grave, cloisters of German cathedrals, and a New York City plot of land at the foot of Broadway?

Figure 1.3
WNBA (now known as WIBC). (Courtesy of National Bowling Hall of Fame and Museum)

Bowling Participation Today

2

Popularity

The popularity of bowling took a dramatic upswing with the introduction of automatic pinsetting devices in 1952 (fig. 2.1). With the construction of large bowling centers complete with lounges, dining rooms, and even nurseries, bowling lost its unsavory "pool hall" association to become one of the largest participation sports and one of the most popular forms of family recreation in the United States. From the fall of 1994 to the spring of 1995 more than 80 million people in the United States bowled at least one game, and another 4.9 million adults bowled in weekly leagues. Forty-eight percent of league bowlers are adult men, 41 percent are adult women, and 11 percent are youth between the ages of five and seventeen. Despite the fact that interest in league bowling has waned recently, the good news is a rise in solo bowling. Bowling centers are becoming total entertainment centers with video games, putt-putt golf, pool tables, and some centers are smoke-free.

The skills needed to achieve an average performance in bowling and to enjoy taking part in the game are relatively easy to acquire. Less preparation and participation time is required for bowling than for many other sports. Because time is such a limiting factor, given the tempo of modern living, bowling is an excellent activity for a busy family get-together.

The informal nature of the game allows for socializing and chitchat between turns. In addition, league bowling affords an opportunity to make many new friends and acquaintances as teams meet different opponents each week. The time between turns that permits relaxation and socializing is balanced by the need for concentration and mental alertness in order to judge pin formations and choose strategies of the game. Bowling offers a constant challenge, and watching one's own ball control and average improve can be highly satisfying, whether you are bowling informally with family or friends or are involved in a highly competitive league.

As a service to increase the awareness of bowling as a sport and leisure time activity and to promote youth fitness in physical education classes, the National Bowling Council and the Young America Bowling Alliance have developed an In-School Bowling Program. The kit contains four rubber balls, four sets of pins, an instruction video, lesson plans, activity sheets, a supplemental math kit, and tote bags. Some establishments provide assistance to young children by placing bumpers made of rubber or styrofoam in the channels (gutters) to ensure that the ball moves down the lane and hits the pins (fig. 2.2). On the college scene, many student union buildings include bowling facilities to provide recreation and league competition for students, faculty, and employees (fig. 2.3).

Figure 2.1
A look back in time—one of the unique exhibits at the National Bowling Hall of Fame and Museum features the lost art of pinsetting. Pinboys, such as the two featured in the exhibit, were a common sight at bowling centers from the late 1800s until the development of automatic pinsetters in the 1950s. (Courtesy of National Bowling Hall of Fame and Museum)

The American Bowling Congress (ABC), the Women's International Bowling Congress (WIBC), and the Young American Bowling Alliance (YABA), (formerly the American Junior Bowling Congress) have stimulated interest in bowling by offering competitive events and free instruction for men, women, and young bowlers. Volunteer workers from these organizations donate their time to teach bowling and to organize and conduct leagues. Television has encouraged thousands of viewers to learn the game, greatly supplementing the promotional efforts of the ABC and WIBC.

Take an informal survey of your community. How many bowling facilities are in operation, and which ones are open to you?

Figure 2.2
Bumpers for the channel (gutter).

Watch the Pros

You can learn strategy and study techniques, as well as see expert performances, if you watch professional bowlers in action. Televised tournaments and money matches have encouraged many skilled bowlers to "turn pro." The Professional Bowler's Association (PBA) was founded in 1958 to promote the best in bowling performance; its first tournament was held in 1959, when many television shows first appeared. Bowling, like golf and tennis, has gained popularity with television audiences to such an extent that not only are the finals of the winter tournaments of the Pro Bowlers Tour, the U.S. Open, and All-Star events televised, but other exciting matches between champions can usually be seen on weekends.

In 1995, a new National Bowling Stadium was erected in Reno, Nevada. The stadium has eighty lanes in a row, seating for 1,200 spectators, and an omnimax

Figure 2.3
University bowling center. (Courtesy of Dr. Agne-Traub's Howard University bowling class)

theater dome. The stadium has the world's largest rear-projection television screen/ scoreboard that spans the 440-foot play area. The facility covers a full city block in downtown Reno and will host the WIBC National Tournament in 1997, yet the largest bowling center in the nation is the 106 lanes at Showboat in Las Vegas, Nevada.

Despite the fact that the PBA is a youngster among professional sports organizations, it already has an established prestige and tradition. The American Bowling Congress has had a Hall of Fame since 1941; only the sports of baseball (1936) and golf (1940) have honored their heroes longer. The Hall was located inside bowling headquarters in Greendale, Wisconsin, until June of 1984 when the National Bowling Hall of Fame and Museum opened in St. Louis, Missouri (fig 2.4). Among the more than one hundred male honorees are such greats as Don Carter, Dick Weber, Ray Bluth, Andy Varipapa, and Nelson Burton, Sr. Marian Ladewig, Judy (Soutar) Clark, and eighty other women are also Hall of Fame members (fig. 2.5). Many of these names may be familiar to readers because they either appear as names of bowling centers across the United States or because sons and daughters have followed in their footsteps.

In bowling, as in other sports, top performers set the records; however, records are made to be broken. According to the WIBC *1994 Media Guide,* the highest three-game series by a woman in a league is Patty Ann's 859 (280, 300, 279) bowled on April 2, 1985. Jeanne Maiden's 864 (300, 300, 264) on November 23, 1986 is the highest three-game series rolled in tournament play.

The first-ever 900 series award in the 101-year history of the American Bowling Congress was achieved by Jeremy Sonnenfeld on February 2, 1997, in a tournament

Figure 2.4
National Bowling Hall of Fame and Museum, St. Louis, Missouri. (Courtesy of National Bowling Hall of Fame and Museum)

in Lincoln, Nebraska. Jeremy, from Sioux Falls, South Dakota, rolled the three consecutive 300 games across six lanes in the Junior Husker Tournament at Sun Valley Lanes in Lincoln. Sonnenfeld is a collegiate All-American on the University of Nebraska's bowling team, and this tournament was an annual scholarship fund-raiser for youth bowlers.

The previous three-game record was Tom Jordan's 899 (300, 299, 300) rolled in the 1989–1990 season in Paterson, New Jersey, to surpass Allie Brandt's 886 first rolled in 1939. Five other bowlers have scored 900 series that were not allowed by the ABC for various rule or lane violations.

According to *The Big Book of Bowling* by Howard Stallings, the highest beginners first game league score ever bowled was a 253 by Bud Terrell of Bloomfield, Iowa, in 1974. The oldest league bowler through 1993 was John Venturello of Sunrise, Florida, who was 105 years young in 1993.

International Scene

Tenpins is played by over 110 million devotees in more than eighty nations. The world's largest bowling hall, with 252 lanes, is the Tokyo World Lanes Bowling Center in Tokyo, Japan.

Figure 2.5
WIBC Hall of Fame. (Courtesy of National Bowling Hall of Fame and Museum)

International participation is not a recent development. In the 1936 Olympic Games in Berlin, Germany, international bowling competition was held concurrently with the Games. This exposure gave unprecedented attention to the sport. However, the turbulent World War II years intervened to limit bowling's subsequent link to the Olympics and even jeopardized the Games themselves. The Games were revitalized in 1948, but it took bowling over forty years to become part of another Olympic experience.

Bowling was an official exhibition sport in the XXIV Olympiad Summer Games held in Seoul, Korea, on September 18, 1988. Each country participating internationally does so through the Federation Internationale des Quilleurs (FIQ), the world governing body for bowling. Twenty-four amateur athletes, twelve women and twelve men, four from each of the three FIQ Zones competed for three medals. The exhibition format consisted of eleven head-to-head, one-game matches. The top three scorers advanced to the stepladder final for the gold, silver, and bronze medals.

The FIQ was founded in 1951 and consisted of eight European countries. *Quilleurs* is the French word for "skittles," one form of bowling popular in Europe. The United States was granted membership in 1961 and first competed in FIQ competition in 1963 in Mexico. The FIQ and the International Olympic Committee (IOC), responsible for upholding the Olympic principle of amateurism, did not sanction the practice of U.S. bowlers competing for cash prizes, merchandise, and trophies in leagues and tournaments. Not until the ABC and WIBC created a separate division for avowed professionals in its annual tournament and established a separate governing body for international competition, open to all bowlers, did the United States meet FIQ, USOC, and IOC regulations. On June 26–27, 1989, the United States Tenpin Bowling Federation (USTBF) was recognized by the United States Olympic Committee (USOC) and FIQ as the national government body for national and international amateur bowling competition in the United States.

Figure 2.6
Bowling appeals to everyone.

The United States, through the USTBF Team USA program, has participated in the U.S. Olympic Festivals in 1989, Oklahoma City; 1990, Minneapolis; and 1991, Los Angeles. The Team USA program has opened the doors to international play for each of the 4.9 million men, women, and youth members of the ABC, WIBC, and YABA.

The United States Deaf Bowling Federation selected a Deaf Team USA to compete in the 17th Summer World Games for the Deaf in Sofia, Bulgaria, in July 1993.

Everyone's Sport

Bowling has gained respectability and prestige over the course of recent years to the degree that has become one of the most popular sports for participants of all ages, regardless of sex, size, shape, or physical condition (fig. 2.6). Bowling is an adaptable

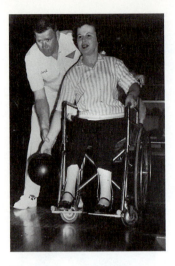

Figure 2.7
Wheelchair bowler. (Courtesy of
National Bowling Hall of Fame
and Museum)

sport because practically everyone can participate. Many persons in their nineties have been active league bowlers, and a few have kept bowling after they turned 100 years old. Disabled children and adults can enjoy bowling, and many establishments provide organized leagues for these individuals.

According to the American Blind Bowling Association (ABBA), over 21,000 visually handicapped people participate in bowling. Most blind bowlers use a guide rail, twelve to fifteen feet in length, for assistance in finding their line. Some blind bowlers prefer not to use the rail, and in this case, the ball return serves as a starting position guidepost. Most blind bowling leagues place sighted bowlers on each team to serve as pin callers and scorekeepers.

Wheelchair bowlers have organized leagues in different parts of the country through the joint efforts of the ABC or WIBC and the American Wheelchair Bowling Association, Inc. The major needs for wheelchair bowlers are accessibility into the bowling center and ramps onto the approach. Most bowlers use a regular bowling ball and execute delivery of the ball by swinging their arm to the side of the wheelchair after the chair has been positioned on the approach and locked in place (fig. 2.7). Some wheelchairs have a ball holder clamped on the arm to enable the bowler to carry the ball from the ball return to the foul line more easily.

Other aids for disabled persons include bowling sticks, ramps, or snap-handle balls. Special equipment can assist bowlers with any variety of disabilities. For example, a person who uses a cane can push the ball down the lane with a bowling stick (most bowling sticks resemble shuffleboard sticks). Naturally, individuals can also make use of their foot to propel the ball down the lane; this is the best means for the double arm amputee to enjoy the sport.

Figure 2.8
Handle-grip bowling ball. (Courtesy of
National Bowling Hall of Fame and
Museum)

Bowling ball ramps are of particular help to the very young or old, the mentally retarded, or the severely physically disabled. The bowler or an assistant places the ball on the top of the bowling ramp, which is centered in front of the lane. The bowler then pushes the ball with their hands, sending it down the lane and onto the alley. The snap-handle, or handle-grip, bowling ball (fig. 2.8) is especially helpful to persons with rheumatoid (crippling) arthritis. This unique type of handle allows the bowler to grip the ball with comfortable balance. When the ball is released, the handle retracts, completely flush to the ball, allowing true roll. The handle grip was developed in 1961 by Les Barker of Chicago, Illinois.

Bowling has proven to be a recreational sport for people of all ages with minor or severe disabilities. In most cases, local competition is provided for anyone who enjoys the challenge of knocking down the ten pins—the young or old, the blind or sighted, the mobile or nonambulatory. The activity of bowling, whether performed well or not, provides a social outlet and a potential means of building self-confidence.

Skills Essential for Everyone

3

Purpose of the Game

Bowling appears to consist of the very simple maneuver of rolling a large, heavy ball down a lane at a grouping of ten wooden pins set up in triangular formation at the end of the lane. However, bowling, as a game, is deceptive; it calls for a high degree of proficiency, is challenging to the most skillful, yet it interests everyone. The object of the game is to knock down as many pins as possible in ten frames. Each frame involves one or two attempts (the tenth frame may involve three attempts), and the score is the total number of pins knocked down in the ten frames (plus bonuses). A perfect game of 300 is scored by knocking down all pins with the first ball rolled in each frame (strike) and then rolling strikes for both additional bonus balls in the tenth frame. A low score in the 70s or 80s may result if an inexperienced bowler needs two balls in each frame, very seldom knocks down all the pins in the two attempts, or receives no bonuses for strikes or spares (all pins knocked down with two balls). For detailed scoring instruction, see chapter 6.

Learning to bowl is largely a matter of developing the concept of toppling pins by rolling the ball at them smoothly and at the proper angle, instead of slamming the ball at them. To accomplish the smooth roll successfully, the learner must abandon the natural inclination to throw the ball down the lane with as much force as can be mustered. This poses a problem to bowlers who like speed. A ball thrown with uncontrolled speed is rarely synonymous with a strike ball. The weight of the ball and the distance to the pins are apt to make the beginner think that the faster he or she rolls the ball the sooner it will get to the pins without deviation and that the more force it carries the more pins will go down. While a certain amount of ball speed is necessary to knock over the pins, excessive speed causes the pins to fly up and off the alley instead of allowing the chain reaction of one pin hitting another pin until all topple over. Of course, it is essential that the ball hit the pins at the correct spot for the chain reaction to produce a strike (fig. 3.1)! Before you ever lift a bowling ball to try the game, set your mind toward the objective of learning to "roll" a smooth, well-controlled ball.

Preparation

Now that the challenge of rolling a smooth, well-controlled ball is firm and clear in your mind, there are a few preliminary steps to be taken before you step up to roll the ball.

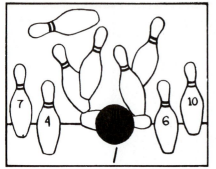
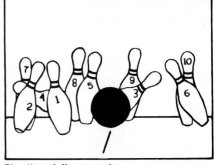

Pins "fly"—incorrect   Pins "topple"—correct

Figure 3.1
Pins "fly"—incorrect. Pins "topple"—correct.

Dress

First, dress appropriately to allow for freedom of movement. Bowling does not require a special costume, although shirts and blouses should be loose around the arms and shoulders to assure an unhampered arm swing. Women bowlers should wear skirts, slacks, or shorts that will allow for the knee bend and stretch in the sliding motion at delivery. Skirts should be neither too narrow nor too full, for either would restrict the delivery, and slacks should not be so long or tight that they prevent a good sliding movement.

Shoes

Bowling shoes are required in all bowling establishments. If you do not have your own pair of shoes, you can rent them at the bowling center. Check out shoes, reserve a lane, pick up a scoresheet, or obtain instructions for computerized scoring at the checkout desk before going to a lane. Pay the fees for the games bowled when you return the shoes to the desk after you finish bowling.

Ball Selection

Take your time in selecting a ball from the rack, unless you have your own ball. Find a ball that is suitable in weight, span, and size of finger and thumbholes. House balls are sometimes arranged on the rack according to number and weight, and in addition may have the weight stamped on the ball. Some houses have balls color coded by weight in pounds. One example of a color-coding pattern follows: 8–9 black; 10 honeycomb; 11 blue; 12 silver; 13 cherry; 14 caramel; 15 scarlet; 16 charcoal. If you have never bowled before, probably all balls will seem heavy. In general, men should select a ball in the 14- to 16-pound range, and women should select one in the 10- to 12-pound range. The regulation maximum weight of a bowling ball is 16 pounds. Lighter balls are made for very young bowlers with no minimum weight set.

Figure 3.2
Conventional grip.

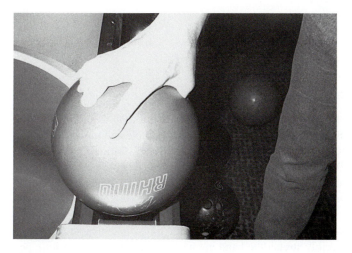

Figure 3.3
Fingertip grip.

Grip

There are three basic types of bowling grips—conventional, semifingertip, and fingertip. *The conventional (or standard) grip is the one that should be used in learning to bowl.* All house balls are drilled with a conventional grip. In the conventional grip, the second and third fingers are inserted as far as the second joint (fig. 3.2). In the fingertip grip, the fingers are inserted only as far as the first joint (fig. 3.3). This grip is used by professionals and above average, experienced bowlers. In the semifingertip grip, the fingers are inserted midway between the first and second joint. This grip is rarely used today.

Figure 3.4
Checking the span.

The thumbhole should be large enough to allow the thumb to slide in and out freely. Test this by inserting the thumb all the way in the hole and turning it rapidly clockwise and counterclockwise. If this can be done with very little friction, then the thumb fit is proper. To determine the correct span or distance between the thumbhole and finger holes, insert the thumb as far as possible in the thumbhole and extend the hand and fingers over the contour of the ball so that the fingers stretch over the holes as shown in figure 3.4. The second joint of the middle finger should extend approximately one-fourth inch beyond the inside edge of the finger hole using the conventional grip. Do not forcibly stretch the hand in checking the span. The marking pen lying on the hand shows that the hand, arm, and fingers are straight from the elbow to the fingers. Left-handed bowlers should use balls drilled especially for them in order to have the correct location of the middle-finger hole. It is set in about one-fourth inch closer to the thumbhole than is the ring-finger hole.

When you have found a ball that seems to fit comfortably, test it by gripping it and swinging it back and forth in a pendulum swing motion, then test one or two more balls and choose the one that feels best. The real test comes in rolling the ball, however, and you may wish to try several balls the first few times you bowl. Be particular and select the best available fit for you, until the time comes that you can purchase your own ball and have it drilled to fit your hand and grip.

A word of caution in picking up the ball from the ball return: right from the start, get into the habit of picking up your ball from the return *with both hands,* to eliminate the possibility of finger injury or strain. Extend the hands on opposite sides of

(a)

(b)

(c)

Figure 3.5
Lifting the ball from the rack.

the ball away from any oncoming balls and lift the ball from the return as though there were no holes in it (fig. 3.5*a* and *b*). Always protect your fingers as you pick up the ball so an oncoming ball will not hit your fingers (fig. 3.5*c*).

Picking up the ball with the fingers in the holes is fatiguing and puts strain on the fingers and arm, and there is a possibility of dropping it on the approach, or worse yet, on your foot.

What are the points to check in selecting a house bowling ball? When you find a seemingly comfortably fit, how should you test the ball?

Basic Skills

Much of your success in bowling will depend on how well you master the preliminary actions necessary for the smooth, well-controlled delivery of the ball. As in any
sport, learning and practicing the fundamental movement patterns are necessary in
order to achieve the best results—in this case, to project a ball toward a given target
as efficiently and accurately as possible. For the average person, there is no shortcut
to optimum performance in an activity involving a ball or an object except to understand and practice the fundamentals leading up to the actual projection of that ball
or object. The preparatory actions, the patterns of arm and leg coordination, and the
application of force, timing, and balance are as important in delivering a bowling
ball as they are in putting the shot or serving a tennis ball. The basic skills required
are the same for everyone, but over time, each individual develops his or her own
style or action pattern.

Note: Keep in mind that most directions are given in terms of right-handed
bowlers. Left-handers should carefully read the directions and make adjustments to
suit their needs.

Where to Stand on the Approach

The starting position can reflect individual preference as long as it is comfortable
and relaxed. There are no hard-and-fast rules on how to address the pins except that
you should face the target squarely, with your shoulders on an imaginary line at right
angles to the target. Fix your eyes on the target or spot for which you are aiming. A
more detailed explanation of spot bowling will appear in the next chapter. The position of your feet and the height at which the ball is held vary from bowler to bowler.
The ball is generally held waist or chest high with feet parallel or one foot slightly
ahead of the other. You may need to experiment with different stances and ball positions before you decide on one best suited to your timing and strength.

Determine where to stand in relation to distance from the foul line. You can
gauge the proper distance by standing with your back to the alley bed at the foul line
and pacing off four and one-half normal walking steps toward the beginning of the
approach. The half step allows for the slide as you roll the ball. Note the spot at
which you arrive. The proper position in relation to the center of the alley varies with
the type of ball rolled. Until you have practiced enough to know what kind of ball
(straight, hook, curve, reverse hook, or backup) you will be rolling, it is safe for a
right-hander to assume a position on the right side of the approach. The general inclination is to stand in the center and roll the ball down the middle of the alley bed at
the center of the pins, but *the strategic angle is from right to left for right-handed
bowlers or from left to right for left-handed bowlers.* Such an angle with slight individual variations allows for maximum toppling of pins. The angle and points of aim
will be discussed in chapter 4 in the sections covering spot bowling and target arrows
(points of aim).

Once you have experimented with several starting positions, have developed
enough control and consistency to know how your ball is going to roll, and know

what path it will take to the pins, you must check the starting position of your feet each time you roll a ball in order to improve your consistency and control. Check your heels or toes in relation to certain boards or the brown dots on the approach. It is essential that you *stand on the same boards each time you roll the first ball of a frame.* The feet should be a few inches apart and on a line parallel with the target or spot, or the left foot may be a few inches ahead for a normal four-step approach. Depending upon the results of the first ball (that is, the position of the remaining pins), you may need to change your starting position for the second ball. Adjustments for the second ball will be discussed under spare bowling techniques in the next chapter.

The key is to feel comfortable, to relax, and to concentrate on the target. To help you relax as you assume the starting position, try taking a deep breath and exhaling slowly, then look to both your right and left to be sure there will be no distractions from other bowlers to upset your concentration as you make the approach to deliver the ball.

The Four-Step Approach

Introduction

The approach is the method of building up momentum for delivery of the ball by taking four walking steps forward in coordination with a pendulumlike swing of the right arm (fig. 3.6).

Before concentrating on the mechanics of the approach, keep in mind that (1) speed is not the essential factor, (2) you are going to walk at a moderate pace rather than "charge" toward the foul line, and (3) you will prepare to "roll" the ball instead of "throwing" it.

The four-step approach, while not the only one, is recommended and used by many top bowlers. If you have tried to bowl without instruction, you may have fallen into a three-step or even a five-step pattern. Unless you have bowled for a number of years using one of these, or a qualified instructor has allowed you to continue an odd-step patten because of your unusual ability or success with it, you should learn the four-step approach because it is more rhythmic than the other approaches. If you are using the three-step approach at present and are not too successful with it, or if you have tried the four-step and get overly confused, try the five-step which allows you more time to let the ball swing back. Both the three- and five-step approaches begin with the foot opposite the bowling hand. It is sometimes easier for three-steppers to change to a five-step rather than to a four-step approach. The three-step is the least desirable of the approaches.

Gripping the Ball

After you have assumed the proper and relaxed starting position, hold the ball in both hands at a comfortable height in front of you and slightly to the side of the midline of the body (fig. 3.6a). While supporting the weight of the ball with both hands, insert the fingers of the bowling hand first and then the thumb. Fingers-first insertion

(a) Starting position

First step—
pushaway

Second step—
start of pendulum swing

Third step—
backswing

Fourth step—
ball and foot reaching foul line

(b) Ball release

(c) Follow-through

Figure 3.6
Four-step approach. (Courtesy of American Bowling Congress)

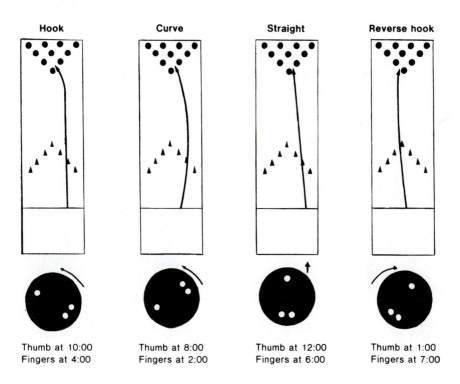

Figure 3.7
Four types of deliveries for right-handed bowlers.

is important because the fingers are responsible for most of the action imparted to the ball at release. Keep the nonbowling hand under the ball and supporting most of its weight (figs. 3.6a and 3.8a).

Men bowlers and the majority of women bowlers should learn the hook delivery at the outset. Unless beginners have very small or weak hands and wrists, or the hook delivery seems terribly awkward, they should start with the technique and the delivery that they intend to use. The easiest way to describe the grip (hand) position for delivering a hook is to drop your arms to your sides. Now bend the elbow of your bowling hand so the lower arm swings up toward the shoulder without changing the hand position. This will result in the hook position of the thumb and fingers. This is the most natural of the hand positions or grips. The thumbhole should be at approximately "ten o'clock" and the finger holes at "four o'clock" (fig. 3.7). Check to see that the wrist, forearm, and hand form a fairly straight line and that the elbows are close to the body. Watch to see that the wrist remains firm and does not collapse behind the ball.

From the stationary starting position, take a trial swing by pushing the ball forward, down, back, and forward again in a pendulumlike swing motion from the shoulder. Try this several times, feeling the ball swinging from the end of your arm.

Figure 3.8
(a) Stationary starting position and (b) first step—pushaway.

Do not attempt to lift or force the ball on the backswing. The arm should be straight and the hook grip maintained throughout the swing. There should be no rotation of the trunk, arm, or wrist during any part of this motion.

Once you are satisfied that the ball can swing smoothly and easily, and have made sure that the V formed by the thumb and first finger has remained on top of the ball during the forward swing, then the more complicated coordination can be attempted. This involves fitting the step pattern with the arm swing pattern. If the arm swing is natural, smooth, and continuous, then your attention can be devoted to the four steps taken in time with the complete arm swing.

First Step

If the first step of the approach is taken simultaneously with the pushaway forward motion of the ball (figs. 3.8*a* and 3.8*b*), the next three steps should coincide with the arm swing action in rhythmic sequence. This step is the most important one of the entire approach. As the right-handed bowler pushes the ball out on a slightly downward angle at his or her side, both hands support the ball until the movement forward forces the left hand to leave the full support to the right hand. You will feel that the swing of the ball outward is causing your body to be pulled forward into taking the first short step on the right foot. If you first think of starting the ball and then move the right foot to make the short initial step almost instantaneously, you will have the correct timing. If you step and then move the ball forward, or even think about the step prior to moving the ball, you will probably be "out of time" and arrive at the

Figure 3.9
Second step—downswing.

foul line before you're ready to release the ball. Persons who hold the ball high in front of the chest for the starting position should be particularly aware of the need to move the ball out just a fraction ahead of the first step. This is necessitated by the longer distance the ball must travel before it reaches the perpendicular in the arc, by which time the second step of the approach has been completed.

Inexperienced bowlers tend to move the body toward the foul line before moving the ball, and carry the ball along on the first step. *Let the forward swing weight of the ball "pull" you into the initial step.* If timing is off at this point, you can be sure timing will be off at the foul line.

Second Step

The ball begins the downward arc at approximately the same time you take the second step on your left foot (fig. 3.9). The second step should be slightly longer than the first. At this point, the ball should be close to and almost parallel with your right leg. If it is not in this position, you either have failed to remove your left hand from the ball soon enough, or you may have released it too soon. In either case, you will probably find that the ball is ahead of your slide or that you are ahead of the ball at the foul line.

Finger position at the moment of ball release determines the type of delivery. Where on the clock face are a right-handed bowler's thumb and fingers if the delivery is a reverse hook? a curve? a straight ball? a hook?

Figure 3.10
Third step—backswing.

Third Step

As the ball swings back and up toward the halfway point of the swinging arc, take the third step on your right foot (fig. 3.10). This step is again slightly longer than the previous step. The height of the backswing may vary. The normal apex of your backswing is usually about the same height in the swinging arc as your starting point on the pushaway. Swing the ball back as far as you can comfortably control it, keeping your shoulders facing the target. Women in particular may not have the strength and, therefore, the control for a high backswing and should just let the ball swing naturally as far back as is comfortable and safe. Increasing the forward lean of your body from the hips on the second and third steps will result in a longer backswing. From this adjustment, the arm muscles are assisted by more of the shoulder and back muscles. As a result, the body is in a more mechanically efficient position, thus allowing the bowler with a weaker arm to obtain the additional ball speed that results from a longer backswing.

The third step is the most awkward for novice bowlers in that the right leg is forward and the right arm is back, a coordination which is in opposition to the more natural right-arm-back, left-leg-forward pattern used in executing most sports skills. However, should you have difficulty with the third step, walk out the pattern slowly and practice it several times without the ball. *Remember,* on the backswing the arm should be in a pendulum motion, *swinging straight back* close to the side. *Keep the shoulders and trunk facing the target.* There is a possibility of a crooked backswing or of overswinging if you allow the trunk to rotate to the right or drop your shoulder.

Figure 3.11
Fourth step—slide.

Fourth Step

The fourth step is more of a slide than a step and is longer than any of the three previous steps (fig. 3.11). Execute the slide on the foot opposite the bowling hand simultaneously with the forward swing of the ball. The fourth step will vary in length with different bowlers and should take the same amount of time as does the forward swing of the ball. Remember that the first three steps were involved with the first half of the arm swing pattern and only one slide step is taken for the second half of the arm swing prior to the release of the ball. The length of slide then actually depends on the speed with which the arm and ball swing forward. Don't be misled by this statement and attempt to rush the forward swing or forcefully throw the ball down the alley. You will not have the feeling of rushing to the foul line if you were "in time" on your previous steps, especially the first one. Still maintain the important thought of rolling the ball off the fingers and down the lane. Make the slide step with most of your weight on the ball of your foot. Bend the left knee, and shift most of your body weight onto the sliding foot. This ensures the braking action necessary to check the forward momentum of your body. The slide foot should stop the sliding motion two to six inches from the line to keep you from "fouling." Make sure that your slide foot is pointing straight ahead and that your shoulders are facing the target (fig. 3.11).

Release

As the ball swings forward to a point beyond the sliding foot, release it by letting it roll easily off, first the thumb and then the fingers. The ball should contact the alley

Figure 3.12
Release of the ball.

Figure 3.13
Follow-through, or holding your delivery
position.

bed in front of the foul line. Have the feeling that you are lifting the ball just over the line. To do this successfully, of course, the body and ball should reach the foul line at exactly the same time, and your arm should reach out toward the target and follow through in an upward arc, elbow bent slightly as if reaching toward the ceiling. At the release, or "explosion point," maintain the position of the release hand—thumb at ten o'clock and fingers at four o'clock. The standard hook delivery will automatically evolve if you concentrate on the foregoing techniques—the correct hand position, thumb slipping out of the ball first, and the entire hand following straight through in an upward arc at the end of the swing. If proper hand position is maintained at release and the ball does not hook, concentrate on firmer finger pressure inside the finger holes as you swing the ball forward. You must feel the ball roll off the fingers last and the finger pull upward at release to give what is known as a "lift" to the delivery of the ball. Note the bent elbow position of the arm on the follow-through in figures 3.6 and 3.13. *It is not necessary to force a hook by twisting the trunk, swinging the arm across in front of the body, or turning the hand over.*

Follow-Through

Observe in figures 3.12 and 3.13 the balanced follow-through position of the bowler at the foul line. The follow-through is as important to the bowler as it is to the baseball pitcher, the golfer, the javelin thrower, and so many others. Any athlete projecting a ball or an object toward a target will attempt to guide that object in a direct line by maintaining contact with the object as long as possible in order to achieve the desired angle of flight. A strong and well-balanced follow-through will also ensure optimum speed of the ball. Novice bowlers who have insufficient strength tend to slow down on the forward arm swing motion even before the release of the ball, with the result that the ball rolls very slowly and is apt to deviate more on its way to the pins.

Study figures 3.11, 3.12, and 3.13 and review the following important checkpoints of the slide (fourth step) for the right-handed bowler:

1. Weight on the sliding foot
2. Left knee bent
3. Sliding (left) foot a few inches from the foul line and pointing toward your target
4. Right leg extended behind the body for balance
5. Left arm extended to the side to aid in balance
6. Shoulders facing the target
7. Body leaning forward at the line so that foot, knee, and shoulders form a vertical line
8. Eyes focusing on the target or spot

Most expert bowlers will "pose" or hold their delivery position until well after the ball has been released to ensure proper balance and position during the ball release. This is a "must" for control, consistency, and high scores. All learners should set a goal for themselves and exaggerate the follow-through by attempting to pose for three counts after release—until the ball is over a certain spot on the alley. Maintaining a well-balanced delivery position after releasing a heavy ball is probably the most difficult of all bowling techniques. Concentrate on perfecting it with every ball you roll (fig. 3.13).

What are the key points to remember for each step of the four-step delivery and for the follow-through?

Summary

Most of your success in bowling will depend on how you perform *behind* the foul line. The timing of the arm swing with the four-step approach cannot be overemphasized. For many bowlers, it is helpful to walk through the approach without the ball while counting to themselves "one, two, three, *and* four," "right, left, right, *and* left." This should ensure that the tempo of the approach is the same each time. The four counts should coordinate with the pushaway (out), downward arc of ball (down), the halfway point of the swinging arc (back), and the forward swing, slide, and release of the ball (roll).

The walking approach combined with the arm swing gives additional force, since the momentum of the body is transferred to the ball. The ball you roll takes on the motion of your body just as you take on the motion of a vehicle in which you are riding. If you step off the moving vehicle (car or merry-go-round), you will continue to move. The ball acquires the same motion as the hand and will continue to move when released with the same speed until it contacts the lane and other forces alter its speed.

Grip

Release

Eyes on target

Follow-through

Figure 3.14

Essentials of hook ball delivery. (Courtesy of the National Bowling Council, Arlington, VA)

Even though accelerating the approach increases the speed of the ball, it also makes braking extremely difficult; therefore, the bowler determines the speed of the approach by the control needed to stop just short of the foul line in a balanced position.

The arm should swing naturally at the side, letting gravity act on the ball to bring it down and back. Leaning forward will increase the height of the backswing, and this lean is also useful in balancing the ball at the top of the backswing. The approach should follow a straight line, since any sideward movement detracts from the forward momentum and interferes with accuracy.

If the ball isn't rolling to suit you, go back and check each of the fundamentals—the stance, the grip, the approach, the release, and the follow-through; better still, have your instructor or an expert bowler check them for you (fig. 3.14).

Straight Ball Delivery

For bowlers who have difficulty controlling the hook or for those who lack strength in the hands and wrists, the straight ball may prove more successful. Though the term *straight ball* means the absence of a hook or curve, *the ball should not be rolled down the middle of the lane.*

The fundamentals for delivering a straight ball (see fig. 3.7) are the same as for the hook. The differences are in the grip of the ball at the start and the hand position at release.

Hold the ball in the starting position in front of the body just as you would for the hook, but rotate the ball so that the location of the thumbhole is at the twelve o'clock position. The finger holes are at approximately six o'clock. This grip allows more of the hand to be under the ball, providing some additional support as you swing the ball. The same "thumb-on-top" grip is also in effect as the ball is released at the foul line. The straight ball will have little, if any, spin; and for the right-handed bowler, it should be released near the right gutter and roll on a diagonal line from right to left into the 1–3 pocket.

Hints for Learning and Practice

In addition to receiving good instruction and reading about some of the fine points of the game, your learning can be enhanced by watching the experts. Watch their various styles of delivery on television, or go to your nearest bowling establishment the night the scratch leagues are bowling, find out which bowlers have the highest averages, and observe them closely. Sit directly behind them and concentrate on their straight-line approach and follow-through, then move to a position where you have a side view of their timing of the steps and arm swing and their body position at the foul line. Concentrate on the bowlers themselves in action and not the pins going down. Also observe their methods for picking up spares and splits. As soon as the first ball is bowled and if pins remain, quickly determine what procedure you would choose for the second ball, and see if the bowler does what you would have done. This mental practice can be used when bowling with friends or watching others bowl on adjacent lanes. Picking up spares will be detailed in the next chapter.

One of the best aids in learning a new activity is the motion picture. Study films of the experts, or have your performance recorded on film or videotape, and compare it with those of the experts. Personally owned or rented camcorders make it easy to analyze your performance.

A good substitute for a visual record of your performance and one that is less expensive is to make an analysis chart. The chart may consist of the key points found in this chapter, or you can develop a more extensive chart to include height and alignment of the ball at the starting position; tempo of steps on the approach; lean of the trunk; height and position of the ball on the backswing; and left knee flexion and arm and hand position on the release. If you will study your completed chart, you will have a definite picture of your performance, and you can note the problem areas that need correction. The chart can be completed by an instructor, or you and your bowling partner can check each other. The process of filling in the chart is beneficial for the observer as well as the bowler (fig. 3.15). Practicing a great deal at the bowling lanes may run into some expense, and it may become difficult to discipline yourself to practice instead of bowling games. Typically, watching the pins fall down and scoring begin to take most of your attention, and you neglect concentrating on fundamentals. Bowling without pins or "shadow bowling" is practically a must for

Diagram the path of *your* ball as it crosses the arrow and hooks. List reasons for your error.

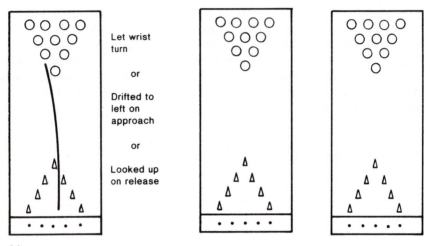

(a)

Diagram the path the ball should take. Use a dotted line to indicate path of *your* ball. List reasons for your error.

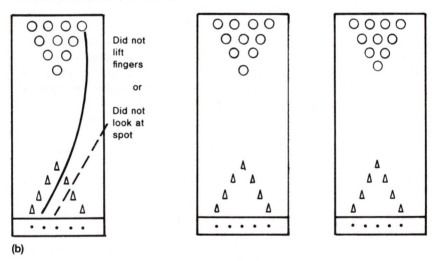

(b)

Figure 3.15
Learning and practicing charts.

proper learning of the fundamentals of approach and delivery. Go to the lanes when they are not busy, and pay your money to just roll the ball for an entire line. Do this as many times as is necessary to develop a smooth, rhythmical, mechanical delivery, then bowl many lines without keeping score. Rerack the pins each time until you consistently hit your pocket.

Practice with a friend and let him or her work on spares (that you leave), while you concentrate on your first ball. To discipline yourself, make drawings of the lane with the arrows and a setup. Chart the path of your ball as it crosses the arrow you have chosen. Note the ball's hook, circle the pins that are left standing, and then write the reasons for your error (fig. 3.15a). In order to diagram the path of your ball, you must keep your eye on the arrows. You will be able to discern if you have a consistent hook pattern; writing down your reasons for error will ensure that you are concentrating on what you are doing. You may use the same type of chart when working on spares. First, determine your strategy and draw the approach and path the ball should take; then after you have bowled, use a dotted line to indicate the path your ball actually took (fig. 3.15b). The two lines should coincide.

Dedicate a few hours of practice by yourself, so you can concentrate full time on the task at hand. Once you start keeping score, make notes on the score sheet, particularly in regard to your spot. You may discover some objective evidence of first or second ball inconsistencies. If possible, try to practice for shorter periods every day or several times a week rather than for long hours over the weekend. Consistency is developed faster by regular practice than by intermittent sessions.

Why is it so important when learning to bowl to practice your delivery without the pins set up?

Prepare a practice sheet with the pins diagrammed for each frame as shown in figure 3.15. Put a check mark through each pin knocked down by the first ball and an X through pins picked up by the second ball. After four or more lines, can you discover any consistency in first ball or second ball errors? If so, what are appropriate corrections?

Skills for Higher Scores

4

Some beginners are endowed with great natural ability and may become better bowlers in only a few lessons or practices, while others may take one or two years to master the fundamentals. Your natural ability along with your desire, motivation, and ultimate objective in learning to bowl will affect the time it takes for you to master the game. Do you want to learn just enough to "have fun with the gang" or do you *really* want to perfect each of the basic skills, learn the fine points of the game, and become an accomplished bowler? If your intent is the latter, then you should allow plenty of time for instruction and buckle down to a good deal of practice. You should feel satisfied with each stage of your performance, and particularly with what goes on behind the foul line, before you tackle the fine points of the game. On the other hand, bowling is not such a complicated sport to learn that the person with average skills can't "have fun" and knock down some pins after only a few lessons and a little practice. This bowler may never get out of the "120" class with this "shortcut" program, but a couple of strikes and spares per line can give the enjoyment, recreation, and exercise that is wanted or needed.

Regardless of the level of seriousness with which a bowler approaches the game, the bowler should first be able to move his or her body and the ball with rhythm up to the foul line, release the ball smoothly, and maintain balanced control of the body behind the foul line. Once the basic movement patterns have been learned and have become automatic, ball control, accuracy, and consistency can be improved. This does not imply that you must be an experienced bowler before working on accuracy and consistency in the path the ball takes to reach the target. These elements are also very important in learning the game. A "better bowler" does not need to think about what the body must do when delivering the ball. The more advanced bowler can concentrate on improving aim, being more scientific in picking up spares, or studying more of the strategy of competitive bowling. Aiming and picking up spares are important parts of learning the game, but these techniques are not considered fundamental. A person could, by instinct or by trial and error, arrive at some way of aiming or picking up the remaining pins, but to become an average or accomplished bowler, one should use a more scientific and effective method.

Methods of Aiming

There are three common methods of aiming the ball to get maximum pinfall: pin bowling, spot bowling, and a combination of the two—line bowling. Each will be described, and you may wish to experiment with all three before choosing one. However, if you wish to save some time and rely on statistics and recommendations of the experts, select the "spot" method. Almost all of today's top bowlers use this method.

Whatever the system you choose, remember that bowling is based on the use of angles. In the proper chain reaction that results in a strike, the ball contacts certain pins, which hit other pins, that subsequently topple the remaining ones. The standard hook ball for the right-handed bowler must "drive" into the 1–3 pocket, breaking from right to left, and make a solid hit on the 5 and 9 pins. The left-handed bowler's hook drives into the 1–2 pocket, breaking from left to right, and makes a solid hit on the 5 and 8 pins. You should select whichever system of aiming will enable you to accomplish the strike most consistently.

Pin Bowling

Using the pins themselves as the point of aim is the least desirable of the three methods because of the distance of the pins from the delivery point. Individuals who are extremely farsighted may have better results with this method, but it is not generally recommended. The pins cover a rather large area. Since the objective for the right-handed bowler is to hit the 1–3 pocket, most pin bowlers will use the dark space between the 1 and 3 pins as the specific point of aim. They should also select a starting position on the right side of the approach and walk in the direction of the 1–3 pocket to ensure that the ball comes into the pocket from the right side. Many novice bowlers start out pin bowling because this is all they see or know. They erroneously bowl from the middle of the lane and aim at the headpin. Another disadvantage to pin bowling is the inclination for the bowler to follow through incorrectly or pull up too soon. The focus should be at the base of the pins to help the bowler to stay down on the follow-through.

Line Bowling

The line bowling system is a combination of spot and pin bowling. The bowler who line bowls usually imagines a black line painted on the lane that runs from the target arrows, or a spot on the alley, to the pins. This line approximates the path the ball should take. This system is often more desirable than pin bowling for the hook bowler because this person "sees" the curved line hooking into the 1–3 pocket. The bowler makes use of several checkpoints along this line and concentrates on these as the ball progresses down the lane.

Spot Bowling

In this method, which is strongly recommended, focus your eyes on a designated dot, spot, or board in the lane about seven feet from the foul line or on the designated target arrow (spot) about sixteen feet from the foul line (points C and D of figure 4.1). Do not look at the pins (sixty feet away) until the ball has crossed over your spot.

This may seem strange at first because you are trying to hit the 1–3 pocket without looking at it, but it works. Plan to arrive at the foul line so that your right shoulder is in line with the spot. This enables your arm to follow straight through toward the spot so that the ball, when released, will roll over this target. Actually, good spot bowlers use several other spots as checkpoints on the approach to make sure they stay in line with the "spot" out on the alley. The spots indicated in figure 4.1 are used for the strike ball.

This diagram shows the checkpoints used by a bowler with an average hook ball. Once you have a consistent hook ball, you will need to experiment with your checkpoints. If your ball hooks more than this, you should pick a spot one or two boards to the right of the second arrow ("D"); if it hooks less, then try a spot one or two boards left of the arrow. You can also move your starting position one or two boards right or left to give yourself more or less of an angle going into the pins.

Either spot method (C or D) has been found to be an accurate and scientific method of picking up-spares, correcting faults, or making allowances for variations in lane conditions.

The Starting Position

Before you make your four-step approach, look down at your feet, and see if they are placed in exactly the same position for every first ball you bowl. The first set of dots at the rear of the alley is fifteen feet back of the foul line and is used by most men and by tall women with a long stride. The

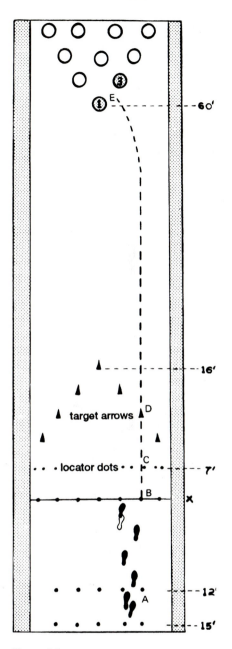

Figure 4.1
Checkpoints for spot bowling.

second set of dots is twelve feet from the foul line and should be used by persons with a shorter stride. Be specific and see that either the toes or heel of your right or left foot are in a certain location relative to one of the dots. Also make sure that your starting position is to the right of center so your hook will break from right to left into the pocket.

Notice that the foot position at "A" is slightly left of the second checkpoint, "B." This allows for the right shoulder to be over "B" at the release point.

The Release or Footwork Checkpoint

Your release point ("B") is actually beyond the foul line, but your hand and the ball should swing over the second dot or in close proximity to it. The "B" checkpoint also helps you to walk a straight path to the foul line during your four-step approach. Take a quick glance at the second dot as you go into your approach because you obviously cannot look down to check it as you release the ball. If you have a tendency to "drift" or walk to the left in the approach, have someone sit directly behind you and watch to see how far left of the second dot you deliver the ball. An even better method of correcting a crooked approach is to check your slide foot position in relation to the dots at the foul line. If you are walking straight up to the line, your slide foot should stop just short of the third dot from the right side, and your slide foot should point straight ahead. Of course, you must maintain your balance at the foul line in order to be able to check the slide foot position at "B."

Locator Dots

Locator dots are seven feet beyond the foul line and may be used to check the angle your ball is taking. Some nearsighted bowlers prefer to use one of these as "the spot" or point of aim instead of one of the usual "D" target arrows.

Target Arrows (Point of Aim)

Target arrows are the all-important "spots" in the spot bowling technique. These spots are actually brown arrows or darts built into the alley. There are seven of these arrows (also called "the range finders") to help you find your range on both strikes and spares. You must keep your eyes glued on your spot as you approach, release, and follow through. Watch the center of the ball roll over the spot. There is a great temptation to look up too soon to see if you strike.

One of the chief advantages of the spot method is that, if you're really watching the ball in relation to a "D" or "C" spot, you can compensate for your aim. Suppose you have rolled three balls in a row that have hit the headpin and left you with splits. You may need to shift your point of aim one or two boards to the right of your original spot or move your starting position slightly to the left, using your same spot. Either move will have the same corrective effect, namely, to eliminate the splits. First, review the key points in your approach and delivery, and correct errors there before making any change. Do not be too hasty in changing your spot. Wait until a repeated error develops.

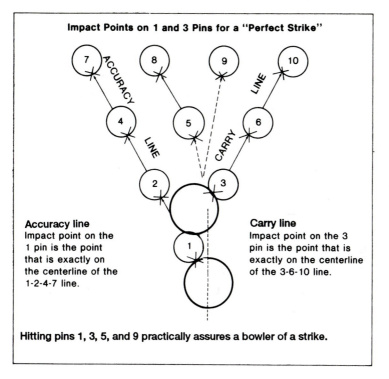

Figure 4.2
Pin action. (Courtesy of the National Bowling Council)

The 1–3 Pocket, or Strike Pocket

If all four previous spots have "checked out," the right-handed bowler should end up with a 1–3 pocket hit (fig. 4.2). This may happen and yet for some reason you don't get a strike. There is a point of accuracy even within the pocket and, depending upon which pins are left standing, you usually can analyze what went wrong. It takes a while to determine which niche in the pocket is right for your ball. In general, if you are leaving splits or corner pins, you're in the pocket, but the ball is hitting too squarely on the headpin. If you leave the 5 (kingpin) or center pins, you are usually too light in the pocket.

Should you miss the pocket completely but hit all other checkpoints (see "E" in figure 4.1), your trouble could be in the ball release. Your approach and follow-through may have been straight to the spot, but you may have turned your wrist too much to the right or the left, or you may have kept your thumb in the ball too long, causing the ball to go straight instead of hooking.

Have you discovered the points of aim that work best for you? In relation to the locator dots and target arrows, where do you stand to begin, where is the ball release location, and what is the position of the ball as it passes the target arrows?

Pin Action

A degree of power (force) is necessary to get the optimum pin action when the ball enters the pocket. The headpin contacted on its right side by the ball will take out the 2 pin, and it in turn (or in combination with the 1 pin) will take out the 4 pin. Four will take out the 7 pin; or the 1, 2, and 4 pins may combine to topple the 7 pin. At the same time, the 3 pin hit by the ball will take out the 6 pin, which will, in turn, take care of the 10 pin. After the ball moves through the pocket, it will contact the 5 pin which takes out the 8 pin; then the ball continues through to contact the 9 pin. On a perfect hit, the ball contacts only four pins, 1, 3, 5, and 9, and these four pins are responsible for the remaining six (fig. 4.2).

If the ball is thrown with too much force, the pins with which it comes into contact are swept off the lane vertically (i.e., they leave the lane in a virtually upright position and do not take out the pins behind [see fig. 3.1]). A ball rolling too slowly also has poor pin action. Such a ball has little spin (from lack of force or insufficient hook) and is more easily deflected by the pins. Consequently, the path of the ball is altered.

With any pin contact, the ball is deflected somewhat, but the ball is much heavier than the pins, and because it is moving, the force exerted by the ball against the pin is much greater than the force of the pin against the ball (see fig. 4.4). From this, it can be concluded that the heavier the ball, the less its path will be altered by contact with the pins. Therefore, it is best to bowl with as heavy a ball as can be easily controlled.

Picking Up Spares

Your ability to pick up spares (to knock down the pins remaining after bowling your first ball) can make the difference between your becoming a low- or a high-average bowler. Beginning bowlers are often so engrossed with the idea of getting strikes that when they miss on the first ball, they hurry the process of rolling the second ball and throw it carelessly at the remaining pins so that they can more quickly get at the next full set of pins. Calculate for a minute the possibility of your rolling a 180 or 190 game without ever making a strike. You have merely to be accurate in converting a one- or two-pin leave in each frame into a spare.

Of course you try to knock down as many pins as you can on the first ball. If your first ball is too far off the mark, you are going to leave pins standing that will be difficult for you to knock down for a spare. However, there are, comparatively speaking, very few leaves that cannot be cleared from the lane by a well-placed second ball. With proper know-how and practice on various spare angles, the average bowler can learn to clear the lane at least 90 per cent of the time. The other 10 per cent of the time may find the bowler faced with "impossible" splits. The good bowler knows to roll the second ball very carefully to make sure that the one or two "key" pins struck by the ball are hit in such a manner that they will knock other pins off the lane. How is this done?

First of all, keep the delivery style on your second ball consistent with that of your first ball. Make only those few adjustments that are absolutely necessary; they should be mainly in the starting position or in the point of aim (fig. 4.3). The type of ball you roll should remain the same; that is, if you roll a hook, stick with the hook on each ball. Some spares may appear rather impossible to get with a hook, but it can be done. Do not switch to a straight ball on your second ball, not even on difficult leaves. If all else is forgotten, plan on hitting the pin closest to you to get your spare.

Likewise, your method of aiming should remain the same on both balls. If you spot bowled the first ball, then do so on the second. Many beginners who learn to spot bowl on the first ball decide to look at the pins on the second ball because it is simpler and less time-consuming than figuring out a new spot or adjusting the starting position so many boards right or left. Actually, the adjustments are not that difficult to determine once the concept of the three basic spare angles is understood; they are the middle spare (5), left-side spare (7), and the right-side spare (10).

As a general plan, to convert left- and right-sides spares, angle the ball across the lane at the remaining pins to give yourself the maximum lane surface over which to roll the ball. Observe in figure 4.3 that the main adjustments occur in the position of the feet at the beginning of the approach, the dot over which you release the ball at the foul line, and your spot for aiming. With this system of picking up spares, the second and third arrows (or somewhere in between the two) are the only targets needed. You may need to deviate one or two boards, depending on the lane conditions and the extent of your hook.

Take time to figure out the best angle for converting a particular spare, and think about which pins the ball will get and which pin(s)

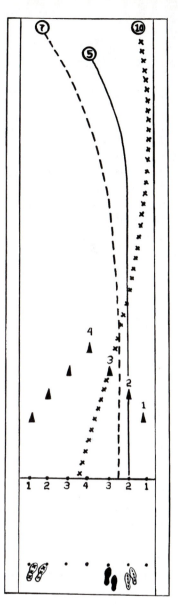

Figure 4.3
Three basic spare angles.

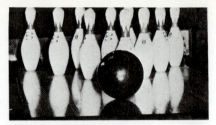

(Top) Light hit—1-3 pocket
(Bottom) Right deviation

(Top) Brooklyn hit—1-2 pocket
(Bottom) Left deviation

Figure 4.4
Ball deflections—right, left.

will topple other pins. In your early days of learning, watch other bowlers attempting to pick up spares, and notice how the ball deflects when it hits the pins. The ball angles quite sharply right or left depending on the approach angle, the number of pins it is contacting, and whether it hits the right or left side of the pins. It does not continue on a direct path straight through the pins. Note the right and left deflections in figure 4.4.

Occasionally, you may observe a bowler, even an expert, who will roll a straight ball at the right-side spares or who moves the starting position and the spot a few boards left for left-side spares. This is done especially if the 2 pin is involved in order to narrow the angle and prevent a "cherry pick" or "chop" in certain situations. This is called "covering" your spare.

The following are a few examples of some common leaves with suggestions for the best ways of converting them into spares.

Which of the following are the main adjustments you should make for rolling a second ball: method of aiming, starting position on the lane, point of aim, or type of ball delivered?

Middle Spares—Strike Ball Position

Figure 4.5a: The 5 pin or "kingpin" is usually left up because of a light hit in the pocket. Try your strike ball again, making sure to concentrate on your spot. A single pin in the center of the lane is one of the easiest spares to get. You have a 23-inch target—combined width of two balls (9-inch width) and the pin (4 ¾-inch width).

Figure 4.5b: This leave is called a "sleeper" and is a difficult one to spare without "cherrying." To prevent this, you must hit the 2 pin quite solidly. For a right-handed hook bowler, this can be done by shooting a strike ball if you move your feet and your spot about two boards left, giving you less angle and decreasing your chances of picking off the 2 pin only. The ball hits the 2 pin, the 2 pin kicks off to the left, and the ball goes back on a deflection slightly right and gets the 8 pin.

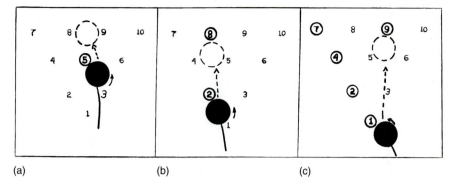

(a)   (b)   (c)

Figure 4.5
Middle spares.

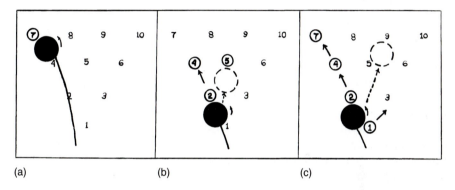

(a)   (b)   (c)

Figure 4.6
Left-side spares.

Figure 4.5c: This is a deceptive leave for the inexperienced bowler. On first glance it appears that a headpin or 1–2 pocket hit down the middle would be the answer. With these hits, you undoubtedly would leave up the 9 pin. Here is where ball deflection is of prime consideration. If the ball hits left of the headpin, it will deflect left after the hit—the 1, 2, 4, and 7 pins will go down, but the 9 pin will remain. A strike ball hitting the right side of the 1 pin will cause a chain reaction of the 1, 2, 4, and 7 pin, and the ball will deflect right and go back to take out the 9 pin.

Left-Side Spares

These include leaves on the left side of the lane with the ball being delivered from the right side.

Figure 4.6a: Begin the approach about five boards or one dot to the right of your usual starting position to give you the widest angle and the most alley surface. Face toward the 7 pin, and walk in that direction on your approach. Release the ball between the first and second dot, and spot the second ("D") arrow (fig. 4.1) or one

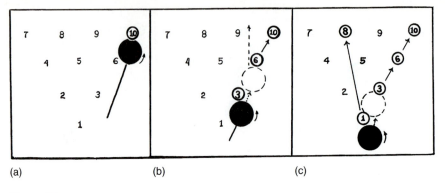

Figure 4.7
Right-side spares.

(a)   (b)   (c)

or two boards to the left of it, depending upon the extent of your hook. Do not ease up on the delivery, because the ball must carry the hook to the last row of pins. The tendency is to get too much angle and roll into the gutter before reaching the pin. Remember, there is more space on the right of the 7 pin than on the left!

Figure 4.6b: This spare results from a very thin hit on the right of the headpin. It is easy to "pick" either the 4 or 5 pin so you must come into the 2–5 pocket strong enough to cause the 2 pin to take out the 4 pin and the ball to deflect slightly right to go back and get the 5 pin. Even if you pull your ball left, you may still hit the 2–4 pocket, and the 2 pin will get the 5 pin. Assume your strike ball position, and bowl between the second and third arrows for a Brooklyn hit (a ball that strikes to the left of the headpin).

Figure 4.6c: Here is a case of the ball not hooking and so missing the headpin. The safest play is a 1–2 pocket ball because the ball contacting the 2 pin will cause the chain reaction of the 2 pin hitting the 4 pin and the 4 pin hitting the 7 pin. Use your far right starting position from the first dot and aim for the second arrow. The 1–2 pocket is not as far left as the 7 pin; therefore, your right-to-left angle need not be as great.

This spare can be converted with a well-aimed strike ball, but this is risky. If your strike ball is a little wide, you miss all the pins, whereas if you pull the 1–2 pocket ball, you may get two or three pins anyway.

Right-Side Spares

These include leaves on the right side of the lane, and the delivery should be made from the left side. Right-side spares are usually more difficult for the right-hander to convert. The occasions when the right-handed bowler must bowl from the left side are not as frequent, and the ball hooks away from right to left instead of hooking into the pins as is the case in the left-side spares.

Figure 4.7a: This is a very difficult single pin to pick up because it is sitting just 2½ inches from the gutter. Start from the extreme left, feet near the far left dot. Face

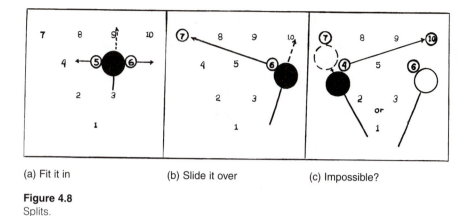

(a) Fit it in   (b) Slide it over   (c) Impossible?

Figure 4.8
Splits.

the pin and walk toward it. Release the ball between the third and middle dots from the left, and aim at the third arrow from the right. Be sure you follow through strongly. If you give up too soon, you will pull the ball left and miss. Beginners tend to get too much angle and go into the right gutter; try aiming one board left of the third arrow if you have this difficulty.

Figure 4.7b: Again, start in the far left position and walk toward the pins. You want the ball to hit the right half of the 3 pin, so you won't need quite as sharp an angle as for the 10 pin alone. Aim for a point between the third and second arrow from the right. Hitting the right half of the 3 pin will send the 6 pin against the 10 pin.

Figure 4.7c: This spare is more of a right-center spare than a far-right spare like the 3–6–10. It requires slightly less angle and the ball hooks into the left center of the headpin. This angle sets up the chain reaction, and the ball deflects back to knock down the 8 pin. Start left of center and aim for the center arrow or one or two boards to the right of the center, depending on the amount of hook on the ball.

The most frequent spare leaves are the 10, 7, 5, 1–2–4, and 6–10. What is the point of aim for each?

Splits

A split is a leave of two or more pins with the headpin down and a gap of at least one pin between any other two pins. A split occurs when your first ball hits too "heavy" or "high" on the headpin.

Figure 4.8a: "Fit-Ins" are so-called because the ball must be accurately placed between the two pins to convert the spare. Actually, the space between the two pins is only about two inches less than the ball width of nine inches. Therefore, your angle must be accurate for the ball to hit both pins. Bowl this from a starting position about one dot left of center, spotting the third arrow. This is a right-center spare and will not require as much angle as a 10-pin spare.

Figure 4.8b: The 7 pin is a row behind the 6 pin; consequently, the ball must hit the 6 pin not only on the right side to slide it over but must hit toward the front right side to slide it over at the proper angle. Bowl from the left side, and spot for the 10-pin position so the ball will hit thinly on the 6 pin.

Figure 4.8c: It is practically impossible to get all four pins unless one pin flys back into the kickbacks and rebounds onto the alley to take out the remaining pin in the split. Try for two or even three pins. From your experience, decide whether the 4–7–10 or 6–7–10 is easier, and pretend you have just three pins remaining. The ball will contact the two corner pins, the 6 and 10 pins, and the 6 pin will slide over and take out the 7 pin. Aim for either the 10-pin or 7-pin hit, so the 6 or 4 pin will be hit thin and slide over.

Taps

A tap is the chief lament of the better bowler because it seems to be a solid pocket hit, but for some strange reason, one pin is left standing. For the right-hander, the most common tap is the 10 pin; others are the 8, 7, and 4 pins. Other single pin leaves are not usually the result of solid pocket hits. Taps are an unlucky part of the game and must be taken in stride. They are not due to the ball action but one pin flying around another pin instead of taking it out. There is little remedy except positive thinking!

Types of Ball Roll

For the average "once a week or less" bowler, the standard hook or straight ball is adequate. Most experts will agree that unless you are doing a great deal of competitive bowling two or three nights a week plus practicing several hours a week, you should not attempt a "fancy" delivery that you cannot control. However, if your ball lacks action or "stuff" so that you're getting very few strikes, you may want to experiment with rolling a different type of ball or get some instruction in that area. You might also try a fingertip or semifingertip ball to aid in getting more lift at the release. If you do attempt a change in style or type of ball roll, you must be prepared to face a drop in average temporarily while you eliminate the old habit patterns from your style and build in new ones.

Semiroller, or Three-Quarter Roller

The most popular of the hook balls and the one that has been discussed throughout this book is the semiroller. It is probably the strongest of the hook balls, but it is the timing of the release with the lift that determines the effectiveness of the hook. The semiroller rolls on a track anywhere from one-half to three-quarters of the ball's circumference. The ball track is the surface of the ball that contacts the lane and can be determined because the portion of ball making contact with the lane picks up minute particles of dust and finish from the lane. The ball should roll an inch outside the thumbhole to about two and a half inches outside the thumbhole (fig. 4.9). The narrower the track on your ball, the more consistently you are in rolling it. A ball rolling

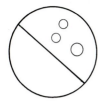

Figure 4.9
Semiroller, or three-quarter roller. (Courtesy of the National Bowling Council)

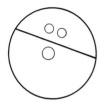

Figure 4.10
Full roller. (Courtesy of the National Bowling Council)

over the thumbhole sounds lopsided and loses "stuff" every time. This is a result of turning the wrist so that the thumb is down at release.

To effect a semiroller, all you need to do in addition to your regular hook ball grip is to lift the wrist upward and inward so the wrist is in a slightly cocked or flexed position at release. The fingers apply the lift (from the four o'clock position) moving upward and following the outward contour of the ball to about the two o'clock position at the time of release. The thumb is turned from 10 to 9 o'clock as *the ball is lifted with the fingers at the point of release.*

Full Roller

The full roller is delivered much like the straight ball except for the position of the thumb and fingers at release. Instead of the fingers letting go from behind the ball (five o'clock position) on the straight ball delivery, they release from the side of the ball at about the three o'clock position. The lift is straight up with no broken or cocked wrist position as in the semiroller. It rolls on its full circumference; the track is not over an inch in width and appears between the thumb and finger holes (fig. 4.10). This type of track is less common since it provides only a minimum amount of power on a rolling bowling ball.

Semispinner

For bowlers who feel a natural inclination to roll or turn the wrist at release, the semispinner may be an effective type of ball. The regular hook ball grip is used, but at the explosion point in the release, the wrist turns counterclockwise so that the

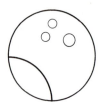

Figure 4.11
Spinner. (Courtesy of the National Bowling Council)

fingers are at about two o'clock and the thumb at eight (a palm down release). The track for the semispinner is wider and cone shaped.

Full Spinner

This is a weak type of hook and is not recommended, particularly on fast lanes. It is released with little or no finger lift and with the wrist turning counterclockwise from a thumb-on-top (palm up) position to a finger-on-top (palm down) position. Since the fingers are above the thumb at the point of release, very little lift can be applied (fig. 4.11). This puts terrific spin on the ball and makes it difficult to control under certain unfavorable lane conditions. The track is very small and looks like a ring at the bottom of the ball.

Reverse Hook, or Backup

This is another type of delivery that is not recommended because of the unnatural hand position at release and how difficult it is to control. It is being described only for individuals (particularly those with weak wrists and hands) who start to develop a "backup" so that they will be able to recognize it immediately and do something about it. A reverse hook may develop when a person learning to roll a straight ball attempts to put more speed on the ball. The individual may twist the wrist clockwise so the thumb is at the one o'clock position at release and comes out of the ball after the fingers. The ball fades to the right, breaking away from the 1–3 pocket, so the backup bowler usually aims for the 1–2 pocket and bowls from the left of center on the approach. This is the least desirable type of ball roll and angle.

Ball Action

If you closely examine a hook or curve ball rolling down the lane, you will notice that the average ball skids about fifteen feet (to your spot), then rolls the next twenty feet, and finally turns for the last twenty feet. This turn begins to take place as the spin motion overcomes the forward motion of the ball. For most bowlers, it should take 2.4 seconds from release point to pin contact. A ball much faster than that is ineffective because it skids farther, rolls less, and hooks very slightly, thus giving little opportunity for the pins to mix. A curve calls for a much slower delivery (but is more difficult to control), so the ball does not skid as much, and the roll turns into a curve sooner, taking more spin at the finish. If your curve quits on you, it is because it has started to turn too soon, and you need to roll the ball farther out on the alley.

Define the term tap. Which pins are most often involved, and is the ball or the pin action responsible?

Hints for Practice

5

By now you should have an understanding of what abilities and achievements are necessary to become an accomplished bowler. The methods you choose for improving your skills are very important. Obviously, the best method is a program of instruction and guided practice with a qualified bowling instructor. The next best thing would be a few lessons on the fundamentals of delivery; some additional reading, study, and observation of what the experts recommend; and then a great deal of self-directed practice. A periodic check by your original instructor will save you time and effort in correcting wrong habit patterns that can develop quickly.

Conditioning and Warm-Ups

Although bowling is not as rigorous as many other sports, the swinging of a 12- to 16-pound weight on the end of your arm for any period of time can be fatiguing to the unconditioned. Before starting out on a "training program" to become an accomplished bowler, make sure you have adequate strength in your bowling hand and arm and a sturdy slide leg. The following exercises are recommended primarily for women bowlers who may lack initial strength.

Improving Grip Strength

1. Squeeze a small rubber ball, such as a tennis ball, in the palm of your right hand (fig. 5.1). Hold the hand in the regular hook position, relax the thumb, and squeeze the ball with the second and third fingers about twenty times, twice a day.
2. Practice swinging a bowling ball back and forth. Use your regular hook grip, and retain this grip throughout the swing process. Try to increase your number of swings each time you do the exercise.
3. Consider some weight training exercises, working primarily with dumbbells to develop the wrists, forearms, and shoulders.

Strengthening the Slide Leg

Walking and going up and down stairs keeps your legs in good enough condition for the amount of bowling done by the average bowler. For beginning bowlers, however, the exercise of balancing on the slide foot, knee bent, nonbowling arm extended sideward, bowling arm extended forward in the normal follow-through position is not only good for the thigh muscles but will help improve your balance. Using an

Small ball

Figure 5.1
Grip strength exercise.

exercise cycle three to four times a week for twenty to thirty minutes will also aid in leg and hip strength and cardiovascular benefits.

Developing the Proper Arm Swing

Your arm swing is important. The arm should be kept close to the body. Develop the same swing forward, backward, and forward again. Practice your swing with a folded towel under your arm. If it drops, your arm is not swinging in the correct path or arc. Another technique is to stand with your bowling shoulder next to a wall, without a ball. Swing the arm back and forth while barely touching the wall with the hand. If you make heavy contact with the wall, your arm swing is not close enough to your hips and legs.

Stretching the Arms and Legs

Warming up through stretching specific muscles and joints can help your scoring and may reduce your risk of injury. Full arm circles can stretch and loosen up the shoulder joint through its full range of motion. Also, crossing right arm to left shoulder while fully extended and crossing left arm to right shoulder can be good for both arm and upper torso.

Bringing right knee to chest and left knee to chest stretches lower back muscles and thigh muscles. Bending right leg backward at knee and pulling heel of foot to buttocks is also good for stretching upper front thigh muscles prior to rolling your warm-up balls. Do this for the left leg as well.

Hints for Practice: Coordinating the Approach and the Delivery

When you do not have time to go to the lanes, practice in front of a full-length mirror holding a rubber ball or a softball. Take your four-step approach, and see how smoothly you can coordinate the hand and ball action with the footwork. Walk toward the mirror as if you were walking toward the pins or a spot on the lanes.

Release off wrong foot   Poor balance

Incorrect starting position   Lack of follow through and no knee bend

Figure 5.2
Common faults.

Specific Aids for Common Faults

Probably the most common errors made by all inexperienced bowlers are improper timing of the steps and arm swing on the approach, poor balance, and limited or nonexistent follow-through at the foul line (fig. 5.2).

Slowing down the approach is a single remedy for one or more of the following errors: (1) forcing the ball, (2) dropping the ball, (3) being ahead of the ball,

(4) charging the foul line, (5) fouling or slipping at the foul line, or (6) delivering a ball that fails to come into the pocket and stays to the right of the pocket. The easiest way to slow down the approach is to shorten the first step (and possibly the second and third), shorten the pushaway, and start the pushaway simultaneously with the first step. Keep in mind that the approach timing—the coordination of the feet and arm swing—is vital to a successful roll. The moving arm should be a free-swinging pendulum. If you have developed a hesitation or if you are forcing the ball, go back to practice swings to reestablish your natural motion. If you have developed a hop in your approach, you are probably rushing your arm swing, or your stance position is too close to the foul line. (The latter is, of course, more easily corrected by simply moving back.) Again, go back to the practice of counting out your steps: *right, left, right, and left* to coordinate with the swing of *out, down, back,* and *roll.*

If you have attempted to slow down your approach but your balance and follow-through are still poor, check the following remedies.

1. On the fourth step, slide with the weight on the left foot, just as you would if you were sliding on ice.
2. Bend the left knee as you slide, and shift most of the body weight to the left foot, lowering the heel as you slide to act as a brake in stopping forward momentum.
3. Extend your left arm out to the side to counter—balance the release of the weight (ball) from your right side.
4. Keep your left foot pointed straight and your shoulders facing your target or spot.
5. Lean forward and reach straight out toward your spot after the ball has been released.

Other Common Faults and Their Remedies

Drifting

Many bowlers do not walk straight to the foul line. Some angle right to left or left to right, and others simply walk in a crooked line, which leads to inconsistency in the roll.

> *Remedy:* Start your approach by facing straight ahead. Note the board on which you start your approach and make sure you finish your slide within two boards of your start position.

Improper Arm Swing Pattern

1. *Too high a backswing* leads to loss of control and perhaps to too much speed for a good working ball.

> *Remedy:* Do not allow your trunk to rotate to the right ("side-wheeling") on the backswing. Keep your shoulders facing the target, and allow the ball to swing back to a comfortable height—straight back in line with the target.

2. *Too low a backswing,* common among women bowlers, usually results in insufficient speed on the ball. This, plus the lighter ball used by women bowlers, makes it difficult to get many strikes.

> *Remedy:* The first thing to do is to strengthen the grip if you are swinging short because of fear of dropping the ball. Move the ball to a higher starting position under the chin, thus allowing more time and a longer swinging arc to build up momentum for a longer backswing. Practice swinging the ball back naturally as far as it will go, and after it has reached the apex of the arc, let gravity and the weight of the ball furnish the forward swing power.

3. *A crooked backswing* causes the arm to swing out too far from the body on the backswing or in too far behind the body; the result is a diagonal forward swing in the opposite direction, and the ball will go too far right or left of the mark.

> *Remedy:* Swing the ball straight back close to your right side toward an imaginary target behind you and in line with your right shoulder. Keep your shoulders and trunk facing your target. Then, swing the ball straight forward toward your mark out on the alley.

Overturning

Overturning or turning the ball too soon results when you try to "put too much stuff on it," causing you to twist or jerk the ball at release.

> *Remedy:* Let the ball do the work by letting your thumb and fingers slide out of the ball easily and smoothly. Make the release a flowing motion. Like the professional tennis player who feels the ball on the racket, the bowler should develop the feel of the fingers lifting the ball as it is released. Wait until the ball has passed your slide foot on the forward swing before you break or lift the wrist. The weight of the ball may cause the wrist to turn slightly, but do not force a turn.

Lofting the Ball

Throwing the ball several feet beyond the foul line causes the ball to skid too much, thus reducing its action. (It usually causes bowling proprietors to wince since it is hard on the lanes.)

> *Remedy:* First check your ball; it may be too light, or the thumbhole may be too tight. Also be sure your front knee is bent and your body is low on the delivery.

Missing Your Point of Aim

If your angle is bad or lane conditions are such that you are consistently missing your spot to the same side, try changing your starting position to allow for more or less angle, as the situation requires.

1. *Missing consistently left* of your spot means too much angle or a ball released too late.

Remedy: Move your starting position only a few boards left, keeping your original point of aim.

2. *Missing consistently right* of your spot means not enough angle or a ball released too soon.

   Remedy: Move your starting position a few boards to your right, keeping your original point of aim.

What corrective action should you take in each case if you tend to loft the ball, often miss your point of aim to the left, or deliver too slow a ball?

Personal Bowling Record

This may be your first bowling venture, yet you may have already rolled a perfect frame (made a strike) and picked up a difficult, if not impossible, spare. Therein lies one of the basic reasons for the popularity of bowling—the ease and simplicity with which it can be performed. The technique of the game is one exercise (combination of movements) repeated over and over again in an attempt to make the pattern consistent. To develop this consistency to the point of machinelike precision and thus to record a perfect game of 300 is almost impossible, which constitutes the challenge of the game, yet the possibility of continuing to improve your score is almost unlimited.

Figure 5.3 provides a helpful way of recording your progress. The personal bowling record is a way of keeping your regular score for a game or series while indicating what pins remained after your first ball. Virtually every standing pin tells you something about the ball you just rolled down the lane. Once you are able to decode the signals, you will be able to make the necessary changes to reduce the number of pins left after the first ball. For example, leaving the 5 pin is usually the result of a ball that is not finishing strongly into the 1–3 pocket (for the right-handed bowler). In addition, the personal bowling record gives you a quick indication of how well you are converting your spares and the frequency with which a particular spare occurs in your game. Recheck the chapter 4 section on spare conversion to help you in this decoding process.

PERSONAL BOWLING RECORD

Name____________________ Date__________ Class__________

<u>INSTRUCTIONS</u>: Circle the pin(s) remaining after the first ball. By circling the pins missed with the first ball, a definite pattern can be established that will enable you to recognize your weak points. Then indicate with an arrow the direction with which the ball hit the pins and which pins were hit first. Cross out with an X the pins picked up with the second ball. A strike in a frame will be indicated by a directional arrow only.

1	2	3	4	5	6	7	8	9	10	extra
7 8 9 0 4 5 6 2 3 1	7 8 9 0 4 5 6 2 3 1	7 8 9 0 4 5 6 2 3 1	7 8 9 0 4 5 6 2 3 1	7 8 9 0 4 5 6 2 3 1	7 8 9 0 4 5 6 2 3 1	7 8 9 0 4 5 6 2 3 1	7 8 9 0 4 5 6 2 3 1	7 8 9 0 4 5 6 2 3 1	7 8 9 0 4 5 6 2 3 1	7 8 9 0 4 5 6 2 3 1
7 8 9 0 4 5 6 2 3 1	7 8 9 0 4 5 6 2 3 1	7 8 9 0 4 5 6 2 3 1	7 8 9 0 4 5 6 2 3 1	7 8 9 0 4 5 6 2 3 1	7 8 9 0 4 5 6 2 3 1	7 8 9 0 4 5 6 2 3 1	7 8 9 0 4 5 6 2 3 1	7 8 9 0 4 5 6 2 3 1	7 8 9 0 4 5 6 2 3 1	7 8 9 0 4 5 6 2 3 1
7 8 9 0 4 5 6 2 3 1	7 8 9 0 4 5 6 2 3 1	7 8 9 0 4 5 6 2 3 1	7 8 9 0 4 5 6 2 3 1	7 8 9 0 4 5 6 2 3 1	7 8 9 0 4 5 6 2 3 1	7 8 9 0 4 5 6 2 3 1	7 8 9 0 4 5 6 2 3 1	7 8 9 0 4 5 6 2 3 1	7 8 9 0 4 5 6 2 3 1	7 8 9 0 4 5 6 2 3 1

Figure 5.3
Personal bowling record.

Scoring and Rules of the Game

6

A game or line of bowling for an individual consists of ten frames. The bowler has ten attempts, rolling one or two balls, to knock down all ten pins in each frame. The game score is the total number of pins knocked down in the ten frames plus bonuses. The symbols for scoring are marked in each frame as follows:

Strike: All pins knocked down on first ball.

Spare: All pins knocked down on first and second balls. Figure indicates that seven pins were knocked down by first ball.

Miss: Failure to strike or spare. Nine pins were knocked down on first ball. The single pin remaining was missed on second ball.

Split: After first ball, the headpin is down and two or more pins remain standing with no intermediate pins in front or between. In this example, the split was converted with the second ball.

Split: In this example, the split was not converted with the second ball, so the number of pins knocked down is shown in the second box.

Foul: A part of the bowler's body touches any part of the lane, equipment, or building beyond the foul line during or after delivery. When a player fouls, no score is allowed on that ball. The detailed rules associated with fouls are explained later in this chapter.

Fill in the score in each frame for the line of bowling shown in the diagram.

1	2	3	4	5	6	7	8	9	10	Total
5 3	7 /	X	9 -	X	X	X	7 2	9 /	X 6 2	

A game of bowling is quite simple to score and involves four basic procedures:

1. *No strike or spare.* Add the number of pins knocked down on the first and second balls; scoring is cumulative.

1	2
6 3	7 1
9	17

2. *Strike.* Ten plus a bonus consisting of the number of pins knocked down on the next two balls rolled. In the example, first frame score is equal to 10 for the strike, plus 7 plus 2, the second frame pin count.

1	2
X	7 2
19	28

3. *Spare.* Ten plus a bonus of the pins knocked down on the first ball of the next frame. Think of the 15 as 6 + 4 (equals 10) for the spare, plus 5 on the next ball for a total score of 15 in the first frame. The score for the second frame is 5 + 0 (equals 5) plus the first frame score of 15 (equals 20).

1	2
6 /	5 -
15	20

4. *Tenth frame.* If a spare occurs in the tenth frame, the bowler is entitled to roll one more ball. If a strike occurs in the tenth frame, the bowler is entitled to two additional balls to finish the game.

9	10	Total
9 -	X 7 1	152
134	152	

Helpful Hints

A combination of strike-spare or spare-strike in successive frames is always 20. Strike = 10 + next two balls. Spare = 10 + first ball in next frame.

1	2	3
X	7 /	X
20	40	

A "double," or two strikes in a row, is always 20 = something (20+?) depending on the number of pins knocked down on the first ball rolled after the double (i.e., 10 + 10 + 8).

1	2	3
X	X	8 /
28	48	

A "triple," or "turkey," scores 30 and is the highest figure that can be recorded or added on in any one frame (i.e., 10 + 10 + 10). Note: This is how a perfect game of 300 can be scored (ten frames of 30, or twelve strikes).

1	2	3
X	X	X
30		

The general playing rules for bowling are few and much less complicated than for most other sports. The ABC and WIBC are responsible for the rules and their interpretation. The ABBA is responsible for rules pertaining to blind bowlers. Space prohibits listing all of the specific technical rules associated with proper league administration, but they can be obtained by writing the ABC or WIBC or by contacting your local bowling establishment.

The following are the general rules of basic play, and scoring and rules of the game.

General Playing Rules[1]

Leagues and Tournaments

Rule 1. Leagues and tournaments must be organized and bowled in accordance with the WIBC Bylaws/ABC Constitution, rules and regulations. These events must be scheduled on lanes that are currently WIBC/ABC certified and only WIBC/ABC approved equipment may be used.

---

1. From the official playing rules of the ABC/WIBC. Reprinted with permission.

Game—Definition

Rule 2. A game of American tenpins consists of ten frames. A player delivers two balls in each of the first nine frames unless a strike is scored. In the tenth frame, a player delivers three balls if a strike or spare is scored. Every frame must be completed by each player bowling in regular order.

Fouls

Definition of a Foul

Rule 5a. A foul occurs when a part of the player's person encroaches on or goes beyond the foul line and touches any part of the lane, equipment, or building during or after a delivery. A ball is in play after a delivery until the same or another player is on the approach in position to make a succeeding delivery.

The certification and inspection committee of a local association can require that the foul line be plainly marked on the walls, posts, division boards, or any other structure in a bowling center on a line with the regular foul line.

Deliberate Foul

Rule 5b. When a player deliberately fouls to benefit by the calling of a foul, the player shall be credited with zero pinfall for that delivery and not allowed further deliveries in that frame.

Foul Counts as Ball Bowled

Rule 5c. When a foul is recorded the delivery counts but the player is not credited with any pins knocked down by that delivery. Pins knocked down by the ball when the foul occurred must be respotted if the player who fouled is entitled to additional deliveries in the frame.

Foul Detection

Rule 5d. In sanctioned competition, a WIBC/ABC approved automatic foul detecting device must be used if available. When not available, a foul judge must be stationed in a position to have an unobstructed view of the foul line. Should a foul detecting device become temporarily inoperative, the following procedures shall be used to call fouls:

1. In tournament play, management shall assign a foul judge or have the official scorers call fouls.
2. In league play, the opposing team captains shall call fouls or designate a foul judge.

Failure to provide for the calling of fouls as specified shall disqualify scores bowled for WIBC or ABC high score award consideration.

Apparent Foul

Rule 5e. A foul shall be declared and recorded if the automatic foul detecting device or foul judge fails to call a foul that is apparent to:

1. both captains or one or more members of each of the opposing teams,
2. the official scorer, or
3. a tournament official.

Foul—Appeal

Rule 5f. No appeal shall be allowed when a foul is called unless:

1. it is proved that the automatic device is not operating properly, or
2. there is a preponderance of evidence the player did not foul.

Legal and Illegal Pinfall

Legal Pinfall

Rule 6a. Pins to be credited to a player following a legal delivery shall include:

1. Pins knocked down or off the pin deck by the ball or another pin.
2. Pins knocked down or off the pin deck by a pin rebounding from a side partition or rear cushion.
3. Pins knocked down or off the pin deck by a pin rebounding from the sweep bar when it is at rest on the pin deck before sweeping dead wood from the pin deck.
4. Pins that lean and touch the kickback or side partition. All such pins are termed dead wood and must be removed before the next delivery.

No pins may be concealed and only pins actually knocked down or moved entirely off the playing surface of the lane as a result of a legal delivery may be counted.

Illegal Pinfall

Rule 6b. When any of the following occur the delivery counts but the resulting pin-fall does not:

1. A ball leaves the lane before reaching the pins.
2. A ball rebounds from the rear cushion.
3. A pin rebounds after coming in contact with the body, arms or legs of a human pinsetter.
4. A pin is touched by mechanical pinsetting equipment.
5. Any pin knocked down when dead wood is being removed.
6. Any pin knocked down by a human pinsetter.
7. The player commits a foul.
8. A delivery is made with dead wood on the lane or in the gutter and the ball contacts such dead wood before leaving the lane surface.

If illegal pinfall occurs and the player is entitled to additional deliveries in the frame, the pin or pins illegally knocked down must be respotted where they originally stood before the delivery of the ball.

Pins

Pins—Improperly Set

Rule 7a. When bowling at a full setup or to make a spare, if it is discovered immediately after the delivery that one or more pins are set improperly, but not missing, the delivery and resulting pinfall counts. It is each player's responsibility to determine if a setup is correct. The player shall insist that any pin or pins incorrectly set be respotted before delivering the ball, otherwise the setup is deemed to be acceptable.

No change can be made in the position of any pins left standing after a delivery, unless the pinsetter moved or misplaced any pin after the first delivery.

Pins—Rebounding

Rule 7b. Pins that rebound and stand on the lane must be counted as standing pins.

Pins—Replacement

Rule 7c. Should a pin be broken or otherwise badly damaged during the game, it shall be replaced at once by another as nearly uniform in weight and condition with the set in use. The league or tournament officials shall determine whether pins shall be replaced.

A broken pin does not change the score made by the bowler. The pins knocked down are counted, after which the broken pin is replaced.

Dead Ball

Rule 8. A ball shall be declared dead if any of the following occur:

a. When a dead ball is called, the delivery does not count. The pins standing when the dead ball occurred must be spotted and the player allowed to rebowl that delivery. After a delivery, attention is immediately called to the fact that one or more pins were missing from the setup.
b. A human pinsetter interferes with any standing pin before the ball reaches the pins.
c. A human pinsetter removes or interferes with any downed pin before it stops rolling.
d. A player bowls on the wrong lane or out of turn, or one player from each team on the pair of lanes bowls on the wrong lane.
e. A player is interfered with by the pinsetter, another player, spectator, or moving object as the ball is being delivered and before delivery is completed. In such case, the player has the option to accept the resulting pinfall or have a dead ball called.

f. Any pin is moved or knocked down as a player delivers the ball but before the ball reaches the pins.

g. A delivered ball comes in contact with a foreign obstacle.

Bowling on Wrong Lane

Rule 9. In normal league or tournament play, a dead ball shall be called and the player or players required to rebowl on the correct lane when:

a. One player bowls on the wrong lane.

b. One player from each team on the pair of lanes bowls on the wrong lane.

1. If more than one player on the same team bowls on the wrong lane in turn, that game will be completed without adjustment. Any succeeding game must be started on the correctly scheduled lane.

2. In singles match play competition, where a player normally bowls two frames each time it is the player's turn to bowl, and the player bowls on the wrong lanes, a dead ball shall be called and the player required to rebowl on the correct lanes, providing the error was discovered before the opposing player has made a delivery. Otherwise, the score stands as bowled, with all subsequent frames in the game bowled on the correct lanes.

Forfeit—Delay of Game

Rule 11. No unreasonable delay in the progress of any game is permitted. If a player or team in a league or tournament refuses to proceed with a game after being directed to do so by a league or tournament official, the game or series shall be declared forfeited.

Approaches Must Not Be Defaced

Rule 12. The application of any foreign substance on any part of the approach that detracts from the possibility of other players having normal conditions is prohibited. This includes, but is not limited to, such substances as talcum powder, pumice, and resin on shoes; also soft rubber soles or heels that rub off on the approach.

What is dead wood and how does it affect the score for the frame?

In the first frame, a player knocks down four pins on the first ball and four pins on the second but steps over the foul line on the second delivery. What is the score for the frame?

Safety, Attitude, and Conduct

7

More than score reflects how much a player knows about the game and how desirable he or she may be as a team member or bowling companion. The player must behave like a true sport and show common courtesies and respect to both team members and those on adjoining lanes. Bowling etiquette is merely a demonstration of everyday politeness and of allowing other bowlers to concentrate fully on the task at hand.

A bowling center, because of its size, numbers of people bowling, and type of equipment, presents a difficult atmosphere in which to concentrate; therefore, respect the wishes of the individual on the lane and remain quiet until his or her turn is finished. Then congratulate the player and show enthusiasm for a job well done; pep and chatter at the proper time do wonders for the morale of the team. Know the personalities and temperaments of the people with whom you bowl. Some can take a lot of kidding or razzing, while others may be insecure and need encouragement.

Priority

Respect the bowler who is on the approach ready to make a delivery. Remain seated until it is your turn to bowl, then move promptly.

Wait until a bowler on the adjoining lane has delivered the ball before you step up to take your ball off the rack (fig. 7.1).

In general, give priority to the bowler on your right if that person is ready to start the delivery at the same time you are. However, the bowler with a spare to shoot has the right of way over the one who is rolling a first ball (unless he or she motions you to go ahead in order to have a little more time to contemplate the spare).

There is an unwritten rule that if a bowler has a split left standing, the player will immediately take the second ball so that the pins are cleared away. A bowler who is about to roll on an adjoining lane may not wish to see an awkward split staring at him or her. Usually if a bowler has a long string of strikes going, that player goes first; sometimes the house will stop bowling and watch.

Between balls, step back to the floor behind the approach to allow the adjacent bowler to proceed without interference.

Who has priority to bowl first when bowlers on adjacent lanes are ready to start delivery at the same time?

Figure 7.1
Timely tip. Do not distract bowler by lifting ball off rack at the wrong time.

Confine Body English to Your Own Alley

Keep your balance and control at all times. Limit your actions to the width of your own lane.

Observe the Foul Line

Observe the foul line in practice games, as well as league games. Sliding carelessly beyond the foul line may develop into a habit that is difficult to break. If you foul frequently, try taking a shorter first step or move your starting position farther back. In league play, an automatic buzzer and light system indicate that a foul has occurred.

Show Consideration for the Lanes and Equipment

Replace house balls in their proper places on the rack after you have completed your bowling.

Check the number of your ball, and use the same ball on the first and second attempts in a frame. Do not roll a different ball for your second roll. The machines are timed to operate during the return of your original ball to the rack.

Check for private ball ownership. Bowling balls used in the game and marked by their owners are considered private, and other participants are prohibited from using them without the owner's consent.

Refrain from blaming the equipment. The fault is probably yours, and you should correct it.

Be careful not to loft the ball on your delivery. Use chalk or dry your hands if the ball is sticking. Lofting also may be due to poor timing on the release.

Help to keep the approaches clean by confining eating and drinking to the area behind the bowlers. This area is usually carpeted and available for spectators. Most bowling centers do not allow eating or drinking in the bowling area by the scoring

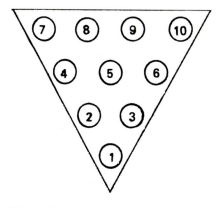

Figure 7.2
Learn the number of each pin.

machine and approach. Make sure your bowling shoes are clean, since stepping in water or spilled drinks back in the carpeted area can cause sticking on the lane. Check your bowling shoes before stepping onto the approaches. Also, be sure the pin machine rack is up before you roll!

Why should you refrain from using a different ball for your second delivery in a frame?

Show Good Sportsmanship at All Times

Control your temper and your language. Constant complaints about bad luck or poor lane conditions are in bad taste, and you may become very unpopular as a bowling companion or teammate.

Refrain from giving advice unless you are asked for it. A bowler who is bowling badly may become more confused than ever. The best advice is "take your time." Play to win but accept defeat gracefully, and congratulate your opponent or opponents for their good bowling.

Be on time for league bowling. You have a responsibility to your teammates, and most leagues penalize latecomers by prohibiting them from bowling if they arrive after the third, fourth, or fifth frame of competition.

Do not waste time. Be ready when it is your turn. Bowlers are often irritated by those who stand too long before beginning their approach.

Double-check your own score and be sure it is kept correctly.

Know the Pins by Their Numbers

To help speed up play, know the pins by their numbers, particularly if pins have been moved or knocked down accidently by the machines and need to be respotted (fig. 7.2).

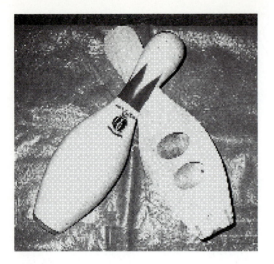

Figure 7.3
Construction of a bowling pin.

The specifications for the size and weight of pins is rigidly controlled by the ABC. Bowling pins usually are made of maple or laminated wood; weigh from 3 pounds, 2 ounces to 3 pounds, 10 ounces; and are 5 inches in diameter and 15 inches high. Hollowed-out holes allow for the variation in weight of the pins (fig. 7.3). They must be unusually durable to withstand the 2,000-pound force of a bowling ball, traveling at an average speed of 15 miles per hour, each time it hits a pin directly. A pin will last an average of five thousand games. Pins are set up in a 35-inch equilateral triangle, and adjacent pins are 12 inches apart from center to center.

The pins in each set must be uniform in appearance, including finish, labels, and neck markings, reasonable wear excepted. The coating of single piece or laminated maple tenpins must be transparent (clear) or white pigmented with the exception of neck markings, identifying symbols, or name. Standard all wood or plastic coated pins shall not vary more than four ounces in each set.

Why is it important to observe the foul line rule even though you are practicing rather than competing? What changes in your approach should you try if you tend to cross the foul line?

Equipment Facts for Enthusiasts

8

Once you have learned the fundamentals of bowling and have become enthusiastic about improving your scores and becoming a competent bowler, properly fitting personal equipment becomes a must. House balls and rented shoes are adequate for learning the game and for experimenting with different weights, spans, and types of balls. However, as in any sport, the caliber and fit of your equipment may help or hinder your performance. By all odds, you will bowl much more consistently with your own ball and shoes. A custom-fitted ball is also much less likely to cause blisters, swollen knuckles, and perhaps even pulled muscles.

Selection and Purchase of a Ball

Weight

Selecting a house ball according to weight was discussed in chapter 3. Before you purchase a ball, try out several house balls of different weights. Keep in mind that lighter balls that fit poorly may seem to weigh more than a heavier custom-fitted ball. In the learning stages, it is best to start with a lighter ball until proper timing and control are perfected and then change to a heavier ball which, all things being equal, tends to get more pins down and stays "on line" better. An above-average woman bowler can handle a 15- to 16-pound ball without becoming excessively tired, but usually a 12- or 13-pound ball is recommended for most women. Some men of slight build or older men may do better with a lighter ball of 14 to 15 pounds.

Fitting

When having a ball drilled to fit your grip, be sure you deal with a reputable bowling manufacturer or custom driller. Some measuring gadgets on the market are not reliable. Remember that a poorly-fitted, 14-pound ball can feel heavier than a well-fitted, 16-pound ball. Many dealers who sell balls employ an expert driller, and the purchase of a ball will entitle you to custom fitting and drilling at no cost (fig. 8.1).

Regulation balls have a circumference of 27 inches and a diameter of 8.594 inches and may weigh no more than 16 pounds. These balls usually have two finger holes and one thumbhole drilled to fit an individual's grip and type of delivery. To be sure all balls meet ABC and WIBC specifications in national tournaments, officials must check the ball prior to competition (fig. 8.2). Bowling balls are checked for weight, density, and balance. A departure from any of these specifications may mean the ball will be disallowed from use in the tournament. The characteristics of

Figure 8.1
Drilling a ball.

the ball may change from day to day depending on the temperature of the place where balls are stored.

A novice bowler may be overly eager to own a ball. Why is it a good idea to bowl for awhile with house balls before making a purchase?

Finger holes became a feature of bowling balls about one hundred years ago. Until the 1880s when the two-fingered grip was introduced in the United States, the bowlers palmed the bowling ball; this is still the practice in duck pins. With the standardization of equipment, holes for the thumb and middle finger became popular and remained so until the end of World War I. At that time, with added competitive events it was discovered that the addition of a ring-finger hole would result in a better, more effective, and less strenuous grip. This three-hole grip still prevails today. However, balls occasionally have a four- or five-hole grip. Many of the top performers today use the "fingertip" ball, but they usually bowl ten to twenty-five games a day and have developed excellent control and stamina. Regardless of the type of ball you roll (conventional, semifingertip, or fingertip; see figs. 3.2 and 3.3), make sure the thumbhole is drilled large enough to allow an easy release. The finger holes must be drilled to fit more tightly to ensure proper release, especially on a hook ball. You should let the driller know if you bowl a straight ball and if you are left-handed, because the ring-finger hole is usually drilled a fraction of an inch farther from the

Figure 8.2
Tournament inspection of bowling balls.

Figure 8.3
Ninepin ball and lignum vitae tenpin ball of Nineteenth
Century. (Courtesy of National Bowling Hall of Fame
and Museum)

thumbhole than the second-finger hole. This is the reason left-handers should not use right-handed balls.

The pitch in the bowling ball is also a very important part of the fit. "Pitch" refers to the degree of inclination the finger and thumb holes have toward or away from the center of the bowling ball.

The more the holes are cut in so that the fingers can approximate a clenched position when they are inside the ball, the more secure the grip feels. The standard for a conventional grip is three-eighths-inch pitch above the center of the ball. Too much pitch can curtail your ability to release your fingers from the ball.

In the early 1900s, the *lignum vitae* (wooden) ball of the nineteenth century (fig. 8.3) was replaced by the hard rubber ball still in existence today. Plastic balls came into use in the 1960s.

Figure 8.4
Bowling shoes and bags.

Polyurethane balls have been popular with professional bowlers since the mid-1970s and are commonly used by league bowlers today. Balls can now be purchased in a variety of colors in addition to the traditional black. To appeal to modern tastes, bowling balls, shoes, and ball bags can be purchased in matching colors and a variety of combinations. However, the softer polyester and the newer urethane balls, while attractive looking, crack or chip more easily and tend to become scratched in brush polishers. A ball with a surface that is too hard will tend to skid, while one with a surface too soft will show wear quickly. Nevertheless, a urethane ball generally will hit the pins harder than a polyester or rubber ball, and that can help most bowlers knock down more pins. The bowler has to decide between longer life expectancy from a hard rubber ball or better performance and shorter life expectancy from a polyurethane ball.

Purchase of Bowling Shoes

Comfortable and well-fitted bowling shoes are another important item to consider for good performance. Bowling shoes are required at all establishments. For a right-handed bowler, the right bowling shoe should have a leather tip and a rubber sole and heel. The left shoe should have a smooth leather sole for sliding and a rubber heel for braking. A left-hander's shoes are made in the opposite fashion. Some shoes are now manufactured with all-purpose surfaces on both shoes. There are many styles, colors, and varieties of material from which to choose (fig. 8.4).

Bowling Bags

Since bowling balls are quite heavy and awkward to carry, it is almost essential that you purchase a ball bag which also protects the ball from becoming scratched

Figure 8.5
Finger grip inserts.

or nicked. (A combination ball and shoe bag is even better.) They can be purchased in leather or imitation leather, canvas, or a combination of materials. Make sure the handles are firmly secured, because there is constant strain on them from lifting and supporting the heavy weight. Double ball bags have become popular with many league bowlers because bowlers may want to change balls as lane surfaces vary (fig. 8.4).

Other Equipment

Although the ball and shoes are the basic equipment, numerous other items are available to the bowler. There are patented grips to insert in the finger or thumbholes to prevent slippage (fig. 8.5). Some bowlers feel that bowling gloves give them better control of the ball. Gloves are recommended for persons who do a lot of competitive bowling or who have soft or sensitive skin and tend to develop blisters easily. Other bowlers prefer to use rosin or towels to help maintain their grip. There are wrist supports to aid the bowler in maintaining a firm wrist position at release.

Many bowling establishments offer a complete line of bowling shirts for men and women. When selecting bowling attire, remember the suggestions mentioned in chapter 3—dress in good taste with clothes that allow freedom of movement.

Lane Conditions

A regulation lane or alley consists of the approach, the foul line, and the alley bed. The approach is a minimum of fifteen feet in length and extends to the foul line. The foul line divides the approach from the alley bed. The alley bed extends from the foul line sixty-three feet to the pit end where the pins are set down and removed by the automatic machines. The channels on either side of the alley bed that catch misdirected balls and the ball return and rack are also parts of a complete lane.

Regulation lanes are usually constructed of maple and pine boards set on edge in order to make a solid, durable surface that will withstand much wear. The first fifteen to seventeen feet of the lane are made of maple to withstand the constant pounding of the ball being dropped or rolled down the lane. It is estimated that 1,800 pounds per square inch of pressure sends shock waves through the lane foundation when a ball hits the surface of a lane. Pine boards, a softer and more porous wood, are used from the spot target area to the pins; their rough grain make more ball action possible. The last section of the lane where the pins are placed is made of the maple or synthetic material necessary to absorb the punishment of the ball contacting the pins. Some establishments have installed full-length synthetic lanes that have a polyurethane base for longer wear.

No two bowling lanes are the same. Lane conditions vary considerably according to the manner in which they are finished and maintained. The surface of the lane is protected by the application of a "conditioner," an oil-based liquid material designed to act as a lubricant between the bowling ball and the surface of the lane. Since bowling on bare wood would be very difficult, the wood lane surface must be covered with some kind of transparent chemical coating to improve conditions. Over the years, the most common coatings have been lacquers, shellac, synthetic, urethanes, and water-based finishes.

Lanes that have just been oiled are called "holding lanes," meaning they are fast and cut down on the amount of hook the ball will take; others may be slow or "running" and the hook will break too much. The thin dressing used on the lanes makes it difficult to see where the previously rolled balls have worn a track. Only with experience and practice can you really determine how your ball will perform on the lanes on a particular day. In addition, each pine board may have a different amount of pitch, and it is the pitch that slows the ball. A reddish-colored board will have more pitch in it than a yellowish-colored board, and it will "take" to the spin of the ball, thus producing a more decided hook. This is also called a "running lane." Increased friction on the lane caused by dust on the ball or on the lanes, or lanes used late in the day after the oil has dried, will all lead to slower lane conditions and thus an exaggerated hook. A "holding" or "stiff lane" is one that is faster and holds down the action of the hook. Lack of friction reduces the sideward spin of the ball and lessens the curve.

In order to adjust to lane conditions, you must move to the right or left of your usual starting angle, depending on how the lane affects your usual delivery. If your ball is not "finishing"—missing the headpin on the right—move slightly to your right to get a sharper angle. The reverse is true if you are pulling the ball into the 1–2 pocket. Move your starting position to the left. Watch to see that you do not move so

Figure 8.6
Lane oiling machine.

far to the left that your body is to the left of the headpin; this is a difficult angle from which to make strikes because of the deflection of the ball. Again, do not change your delivery until you are sure you have read the lane correctly.

A machine is used for oiling the lanes (fig. 8.6). This machine is usually set to travel three-quarters of the way down the lane starting from the foul line. Oil is dispersed from underneath as the machine slowly moves down the lane. Upon reaching the preset distance, the machine stops and returns to the foul line. At that time, an attendant moves it to the neighboring lane where the process is repeated until all lanes have been oiled. Generally, oiling takes place at least once a day. Proprietors use lane dressing (oil) to protect the surface of the bowling lane. Three units of oil (or a covering of approximately 21 millionths of an inch) became the minimum standard set by ABC and WIBC on January 1, 1992. The dressing must be applied in a manner that conforms to ABC/WIBC specifications. In the early 1950s before the present-day automatic lane maintenance machine was developed, bowling establishments had to spray the lanes with a conditioner using a hand-held spray can while moving slowly down each lane. After spraying, a rotary buffer machine was required to properly distribute the hand-sprayed liquid. This process took a long time, and many establishments would dress their lanes only a few times each week. The first automatic lane maintenance machine was developed around 1960, and the present machine shown in figure 8.6 was developed around 1980.

How can you compensate for the effect on your normal hook of a holding lane or of a running lane?

League Bowling

9

Once you have learned the fundamental bowling techniques from a competent instructor and have practiced to the extent that you have a reasonable amount of consistency in the delivery of the ball, you may wish to try out your talents in a recreational or competitive situation. If you desire league competition, check the various league averages at your local bowling establishment to find a league best suited to your current performance level.

Bowling Opportunities

Students in many of the larger colleges and universities have an excellent opportunity to learn bowling and to compete in intramural leagues on their own campuses. The modern college student union buildings include bowling lanes as part of the total campus recreation for students, faculty, and employees. The easiest procedure is to enroll in a bowling class in the physical education department, learn or review the proper techniques from a qualified instructor, and get acquainted with various types of bowling competition offered by the class. Here you have the advantage of bowling with people of your own age and ability and with whom you can become quite well acquainted. This lets you break into competition in a relaxed atmosphere.

Next, you may wish to consider entering an intramural or student union tournament as a member of a fraternity or dormitory team. These usually are handicap tournaments where, in order to equalize the competition, bowlers are given a handicap (see "Terms Relating to Scoring" in chapter 13).

If there is no opportunity for you to bowl on campus, try a commercial lane. There are commercial lanes in the vicinity of most college communities. Many types of leagues or tournaments are in operation both during the winter and in the summer. Some fraternal organizations like the Elks or Moose lodges have bowling centers open to public use. Community recreation programs occasionally sponsor short-term bowling leagues or programs for youth, seniors, and people with disabilities.

League Bowling

Leagues are established at the request of church groups, commercial and business groups, industrial organizations, and other occupational groups. These usually are handicap leagues, although most bowling centers have at least one "scratch" league for the more advanced men and women bowlers.

Figure 9.1
League bowlers.

Organized league bowling is ordinarily sanctioned by the ABC for men, the WIBC for women, and the YABA for boys and girls. Persons bowling in such leagues must pay a small fee to join the ABC, the WIBC, or YABA, and they can establish an official average with the organization.

League teams are usually made up of four or five bowlers, but two- and three-person teams and mixed bowling teams are also common (fig. 9.1). Teams usually bowl once a week, with each team member rolling three games per series. Therefore, a team could win a maximum of three games for that day. However, some leagues choose to play a four-point system, in which each game counts as a point and the total pin count counting as a point. A team could win two games by a slim margin but lose the third game by enough of a margin to make them lose the total pin count, resulting in an even (or two-point to two-point) finish for that week.

A variety of point systems are used by leagues. Some leagues use a person to person match play system. In this case, bowler 1 on team A is matched against bowler 1 on team B. Points are awarded for each bowler's game score over his or her opponent. In a five-person league, each game could result in a maximum of five points per game if team A's bowlers defeated each bowler on team B.

League standings are listed by points won and lost, as well as total pins accumulated each week. In case of a tie at the end of the league season, various procedures can be used. Some leagues have a roll-off between the tied teams, while other leagues choose the team with the greatest pin count as winner. There can be other league variations as long as the majority of teams agree with the recommended procedures at the start of the season.

Handicap Leagues

Leagues establish handicaps to equalize teams with bowlers of varying ability. There are various methods of computing handicaps; two common practices will be detailed here. One system is based on two-thirds of the difference between the bowler's present average and 190. For example, a bowler with an average score of 145 would have a handicap of 30 (190 minus 145 is 45; two-thirds of 45 is 30). This handicap may change from week to week as new scores are averaged in. The second method, recommended by the ABC, uses 75 per cent of the difference between the bowler's average (over eighteen to twenty-one games) and a scratch score determined by the participating league. Leagues for men often use a 200 scratch score, while leagues for women frequently use a 180 scratch score. A man with a 200 average or a woman with a 180 average is called a "scratch bowler," which indicates he or she does not have a handicap. The following table gives the handicap for any participant who has an established average between 100 and 199:

Handicap Table—Scratch 200
75%

Average	Handicap	Average	Handicap	Average	Handicap	Average	Handicap
199	0	174	19	149	38	124	57
198	1	173	20	148	39	123	57
197	2	172	21	147	39	122	58
196	3	171	21	146	40	121	59
195	3	170	22	145	41	120	60
194	4	169	23	144	42	119	60
193	5	168	24	143	42	118	61
192	6	167	24	142	43	117	62
191	6	166	25	141	44	116	63
190	7	165	26	140	45	115	63
189	8	164	27	139	45	114	64
188	9	163	27	138	46	113	65
187	9	162	28	137	47	112	66
186	10	161	29	136	48	111	66
185	11	160	30	135	48	110	67
184	12	159	30	134	49	109	68
183	12	158	31	133	50	108	69
182	13	157	32	132	51	107	69
181	14	156	33	131	51	106	70
180	15	155	33	130	52	105	71
179	15	154	34	129	53	104	72
178	16	153	35	128	54	103	72
177	17	152	36	127	54	102	73
176	18	151	36	126	55	101	74
175	18	150	37	125	56	100	75

The following table gives the handicap for any participant who has an established average between 80 and 179.

Handicap Table—Scratch 180
75%

Average	Handicap	Average	Handicap	Average	Handicap	Average	Handicap
179	0	154	19	129	38	104	57
178	1	153	20	128	39	103	57
177	2	152	21	127	39	102	58
176	3	151	21	126	40	101	59
175	3	150	22	125	41	100	60
174	4	149	23	124	42	99	60
173	5	148	24	123	42	98	61
172	6	147	24	122	43	97	62
171	6	146	25	121	44	96	63
170	7	145	26	120	45	95	63
169	8	144	27	119	45	94	64
168	9	143	27	118	46	93	65
167	9	142	28	117	47	92	66
166	10	141	29	116	48	91	66
165	11	140	30	115	48	90	67
164	12	139	30	114	49	89	68
163	12	138	31	113	50	88	69
162	13	137	32	112	51	87	69
161	14	136	33	111	51	86	70
160	15	135	33	110	52	85	71
159	15	134	34	109	53	84	72
158	16	133	35	108	54	83	72
157	17	132	36	107	54	82	73
156	18	131	36	106	55	81	74
155	18	130	37	105	56	80	75

Using a scratch score of 190 and 75 percent of the difference, what would the handicaps be for averages of 135, 140, and 165?

A typical score sheet for a handicap league demonstrates how the system enables individuals and teams with different levels of ability to compete (fig. 9.2).

At the beginning of each game, the captain adds the handicaps for his or her team. The Saints had a total team handicap of 90, and the Rockies' team handicap was 150. The team with the smaller handicap would be the better team of bowlers, although the handicap will equalize the teams. At the conclusion of the game, the final scores for the team members are totaled, and that total is added to the team's total handicap. As each bowler finishes the tenth frame, the team score is tallied on

TEAMS: SAINTS VS. ROCKIES

NAME	HDCP.	1	2	3	4	5	6	7	8	9	10	TOTAL
Rich	44	7/	9/	7/	6 2	8–	☒	⊗–	7 2	8 0	☒ 9/	121
		8	25	41	49	57	75	83	92	101	121	
Myers	27	9–	G9	7 2	6/	9/	☒	8 0	6/	7 2	7–	256
		9	18	27	46	66	86	102	119	128	135	
Kob	19	☒	7/	☒	4 4	9/	8/	6 3	8/	7 2	5/ ☒	411
		20	40	58	66	84	100	109	126	135	155	
Miller	0	9/	☒	☒	☒	9/	9–	☒	8/	☒	5/ ☒	
TOTAL	90	20	50	79	99	118	127	146	155	175	195	606
Saints Rockies	⑥	2/6	5/8	9/9	12/12	15/13	18/16	20/18	22/19	23/21		+90 696
Locke	53	1–	4/ ☒		8/	3 4	7 1	8/	3 5	1/	6–	105
		1	21	41	54	61	69	82	90	99	105	
Tanner	49	6 1	5 2	G 5	5/	6 3	6/	☒	9/	9/	7 2	234
		7	14	19	35	44	64	84	103	120	129	
Koone	35	8/	8/	6 3	8/	7/	☒	7 2	☒	7 2	9/ ☒	374
		9	18	27	44	64	83	92	111	120	140	
Lacey	13	8/	7/	9–	8 1	☒	5/	9–	6 2	7/	☒ 9/	
TOTAL	150	17	36	45	54	74	93	102	110	130	150	524
												+150 674

Figure 9.2
Sample score sheet.

a cumulative basis. In our example, the Saints defeated the Rockies by a score of 696 pins to 674 pins.

Reading the "Marks"

An indication of the progressive competition between teams during a game is provided by a system of "marking." Marks are given to indicate the difference in handicaps between the teams. Each mark represents ten pins. Six marks, as indicated by the number in the circle on the score sheet, were given to the Rockies at the beginning of

	1	2	3	4
PAT	X	8 /	X	X
KAY	7 /	3 6	0 3	9 /
TOTAL MARKS	2	2	2	5

the game to account for the sixty-pin difference in team handicaps. Subsequently, a running account of the game from frame to frame is recorded by totaling cumulative marks, either strikes or spares. This system enables the bowlers, by counting team marks, to approximate how close the teams are during any frame.

There are three basic rules to follow in figuring marks:

1. One mark is given for each single strike or spare.
2. Two marks are given for each consecutive strike.
3. Marks are *lost* if an individual fails to knock over at least five pins—with the first ball following a spare.
   with the first ball following a multiple strike.
   with both balls in a frame.
   with both balls following a strike.

In the example, both Pat and Kay get marks for the first frame (one for the strike and one for the spare). In the second frame, Pat adds a mark, but Kay loses a mark since her first ball following her spare got only three pins; therefore, the total number of marks after two frames for this team is two. In the third frame, Pat again gets one mark and Kay loses one because she did not total at least five pins in that frame, so the total marks after three frames is two. For the fourth frame, Pat gets two marks for her consecutive strikes, and Kay gets one for the spare. There was no loss, so the total marks through four frames is five.

Even though this system of marking is used and the final marks are even or very close, the final score may vary as much as forty to fifty pins. This would occur if one team consistently had a higher pin count on its spares and total pins in a frame. Computerized scoring shows the actual total (the total including the handicap) frame by frame, so a team always knows how it is performing relative to the opposing team. The computer does not use the marking system since it adds the actual score frame by frame.

Scratch League and Open Play Bowling

In addition to handicap leagues, there are opportunities for "open" play and "scratch" leagues. In scratch leagues, there is no restriction on the basis of average, and there are no handicaps. Teams are credited only with the pins knocked down. Open play bowling provides time for practice or leisure time activity with family or friends.

Leagues for women or housewives and for senior citizens are popular during the morning and early afternoon hours. Junior leagues for boys and girls are available on Saturday mornings or after school. Since most of the evening hours during the week are reserved for league bowling, it is always wise to inquire about the hours the lanes are available for open bowling or to phone to find out if it is possible to reserve a lane for practice or for an informal game.

What is the purpose in recording marks on the score sheet, and how is the starting number of marks for a team determined?

Bowling Strategy

As in other sports, the strategy of the game depends on the situation. If you are bowling an important team match where each pin down is vital, you may use a different strategy than you would in an informal game with friends. In the latter situation where your performance affects only yourself, you may take many more chances in converting difficult splits than you would if your team was depending on you.

One of the first things you can do is to study the tournament temperament and how the individuals on the opposing team react to pressure. Some bowlers thrive on competition; others get to a point where they cannot relax. Some are great front-runners and are terrific as long as they are in the lead, but as soon as someone catches up with them, they fall apart. Others get better under pressure and need to be behind to throw a relaxed ball. These are the strong finishers. Study the psychological strategy first; some later decisions may depend on how well you know your opponents.

Another important part of bowling strategy is making decisions on how to bowl against splits. If you happen to draw a split (or even a large cluster of pins) after a strike, be certain to "count" down as many pins as possible because each extra pin down counts both for itself and as part of the bonus. Always be very careful after a strike, and do your best to strike again or at least hit the pocket and get a big count. In figure 9.2, for example, Rich's total score would have been 123 if he had knocked down one pin on his second ball in the seventh frame.

In most situations after a split occurs, play it safe and attempt to get one pin of two, or two of three. If you are the last player and the game or match depends on your conversion, then of course you must make that attempt. Many a game is won or lost by a pin or two. Never try to convert the "railroads" (7–10, 4–6, 7–9, etc.) by sliding one pin into another. Your chances of succeeding are remote, and you will often miss both pins by trying to hit one lightly on the side. Again, if you need to "go for broke" in this situation, your chances are better if you roll the ball into one pin solidly and slam it into the cushion, and hope it will fly back into the other pin.

Understand the importance of the "ninth frame" strategy. Try your best to strike in the ninth so you can lay a foundation and develop a relaxed feeling for your tenth frame. Remember, with two extra balls it is possible to "turkey out" in the tenth.

Keep in mind that bowling has one of the longest seasons of all sports, usually lasting thirty-two to thirty-six weeks from September through May. Therefore, slumps are inevitable and individual determination and support from teammates are important. One last bit of advice, and one of the keys for team success, is that you

Table 9.1   Averages of Detroit's League Bowlers during 1994–1995 Season

Average	Male (ABC) Bowlers	Female (WIBC) Bowlers
Most Common Average	168.5 Right-handed	138.8 Right-handed
	173.5 Left-handed	142.7 Left-handed
171 and above	50.5%	4.2%
140 and below	9.5%	52.4%

be "strategic" with yourself. Relax, concentrate, take "the bitter with the better," and work toward being a dependable, consistent bowler. Your value to the team will be much greater with these attributes than if you are an erratic, temperamental individual who bowls 220 one game and 120 the next.

In an important team match, what is the recommended strategy for bowling against a split and why?

Compare Your Average

Occasionally, the ABC and the WIBC survey their league bowlers to determine the most common average of all bowlers in the country and from that establish a composite average. Up to this time, only five surveys have been conducted in the United States, the most recent in 1994–1995. Table 9.1 gives the number and percentage of bowlers from the Greater Detroit Bowling Association and the Detroit Women's Bowling Association during the 1994–1995 season. The statistics were provided through the cooperation of the league secretaries and bowlers from this popular bowling city. In fact, Detroit's women's and men's associations are the world's largest associations.

As noted in table 9.1, 94 per cent of the women were right-handed, and their mean average was 138.8; the remaining 6 per cent, the left-handed bowlers, had a mean average of 142.7. Ninety-one per cent of the men were right-handed and had a mean average of 168.5, and the remaining left-handed 9 per cent averaged 173.5.

People who bowl regularly in leagues have been improving their averages over the years. In 1975, only 0.8 per cent of the women averaged 171 or higher, while 26.4 per cent of the men achieved that level. In 1995, 4.2 per cent of the women achieved averages 171 or above and 50 per cent of the men achieved averages 171 or above. Another interesting fact is that in 1975, 21.4 percent of the men had an average of 140 or below, while 56.7 percent of the women were 140 or below. In 1995, only 9.5 per cent of the men averaged 140 or below and 52.4 per cent of the women averaged 140 or below.

Table 9.2   Averages of Detroit's League Bowlers during 1994–1995 Season

Range of Averages	Male (ABC) Bowlers Number/Percentage	Female (WIBC) Bowlers Number/Percentage
>210	1,019 = 1.1	17 = .02
201–210	3,357 = 3.6	57 = .09
191–200	8,757 = 9.3	205 = .3
181–190	15,428 = 16.4	540 = .8
171–180	18,948 = 20.1	1,843 = 2.9
161–170	16,603 = 17.6	4,743 = 7.5
151–160	12,655 = 13.4	9,332 = 14.8
141–150	8,352 = 8.8	13,218 = 21.0
131–140	5,075 = 5.4	13,065 = 20.7
121–130	2,485 = 2.6	10,120 = 16.1
<121	1,376 = 1.4	9,742 = 15.5
	94,055	62,882

Among these Detroit bowlers, the groups that accounted for the greatest number of bowlers was the 31–35 age group for men and the 36–40 age group for women.

From these data and by monitoring your scores, you can compare your progress relative to other league bowlers. Eventually, you too can increase your average and possibly become a member of the group averaging 171 or above.

Understanding Mechanical Malfunctions

10

Today's bowlers are frequently impatient sports participants who get upset when their lane malfunctions. Often the difficulty arises because of some error on the bowler's part, or the problem may be simply a matter of their impatience. The machinery at the back of each lane is a very intricate system of gears, belts, and motors. Constant maintenance is given to each lane in the majority of establishments across the country. Prior to the development of the automatic pinsetting machine in the 1950s, bowling establishments used pinboys for clearing the lanes, returning the balls, and resetting the pins. Today, bowlers rely on technicians to solve the mechanical breakdowns that occur from time to time. All bowling participants who take their event seriously will want to gain a deeper appreciation and understanding of the inner workings of the pinsetting machines that enable them to have hours of enjoyment on a weekly basis.

The photographs in this chapter will introduce the reader to the fundamentals of the Brunswick machines found in many establishments and to the malfunctions that commonly occur on the lanes. Twenty-one pins circulate in the back of each lane; ten are placed on the lane, and the remaining eleven are directed toward their positions for the next full frame. Each pin comes up a conveyor belt as shown in figure 10.1, and when it reaches the top of the conveyor, it drops into one of ten bins (fig. 10.2) that revolve in a circular fashion. The twenty-first pin speeds up the process of filling

Figure 10.1
Pin coming up conveyor belt.

Figure 10.2
Pin entering bin.

Figure 10.3
Revolving basket with individual bins for pins.

Figure 10.4
Pin deck with specified circle for each pin.

Figure 10.5
Complete set of pins on spot.

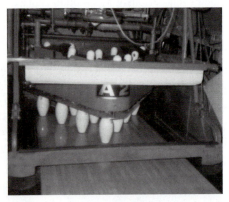

Figure 10.6
Pins on spot with machine in down position.

the basket in case of "dead wood" in the gutter or a stray pin in the back. Like a lazy Susan, the basket with the individual bins rotates (fig. 10.3), waiting to receive each pin until ten have entered. When the basket is full, a lever allows the rack to be lowered onto the pin deck. On the pin deck, which is the very end of the lane, are ten darkened circles, painted to indicate where each pin should be set (fig. 10.4). The exact placement of each pin on its "spot" is important since much of the malfunctioning that occurs is due to pin misplacement. Misplacement may occur as a result of pin action from the ball or from faulty machinery pickup and resettlement. In figure 10.5, the complete set of ten pins sits in proper placement

Figure 10.7
Out-of-range malfunction.

Figure 10.8
"Dead wood" on the lane.

without the machinery visible. Figure 10.6 shows a complete set of pins on their spots with the machine in the down position and the sweep bar in the ready position to remove any dead wood (fallen pins on the lanes or in the gutter). At the top is the revolving basket empty of pins since they were just spotted; the other pins are on the conveyor belt in the rear. Sometimes the pins are moved off the spot, and this causes the rack to land on top of the pins (fig. 10.7). This malfunction is termed "out-of-range," meaning that the pins are off their designated spots, and therefore, the rack is unable to pick up the pins. Movement is stopped when the rack touches the pin top.

Another malfunction already alluded to is "dead wood" on the lanes (fig. 10.8). This expression describes fallen pins found on the lane but for some reason not swept away by the pin sweep bar. These fallen pins give the appearance of being "dead," since they remain lying on the lanes, and they must be removed before the next ball can be rolled. Dead wood is discussed as part of the legal pinfall rules found in chapter 6 of this book. The pinsetting machine goes through a 360-degree cycle in the process of picking up pins and setting them down. Unfortunately, there are occasional malfunctions where the pins get hung up while going through this cycle. In figure 10.9, it appears the pins are hanging from the roof and, indeed, they are midway in the complete cycle. This malfunction is termed a 180, referring to half of 360. This is the most frequent of the cycling malfunctions and only requires the bowler to inform the control desk personnel. They will notify the technician by calling back, usually through an intercom system, that there has been, for example, "a 180 on lane 23."

A variation of the 180 malfunction is shown in figure 10.10. The machine is down, and it is either a 90-degree or 270-degree malfunction since the cycle has either just begun or was almost completed when the malfunction occurred. This does not occur as frequently as a 180, but nevertheless, it does cause a delay which can

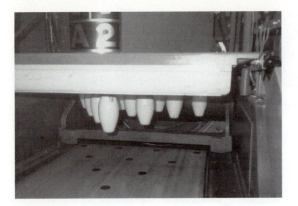

Figure 10.9
A 180 malfunction.

Figure 10.10
A 90 or 270 malfunction.

be irritating to the bowler. Whenever any malfunction occurs, a bowler is wise to use the extra time to concentrate on the procedure to be used with the upcoming ball. Using the trouble button at the scoring table, contact the control desk to notify the technician of the particular problem. Bowlers should let the technician handle the minor inconveniences and not let the malfunction interrupt their concentration on the task at hand.

Computers and Bowling

11

When the novice or league bowler goes bowling for practice or leisure recreation, the player usually pays for each game of bowling. Bowlers traditionally roll games in multiples of three, and averages are also computed on the basis of the three-game set. Now with the advent of microcomputers, a new dimension has been added to the sport at some establishments—bowling by time instead of by the game. Time bowling allows a bowler to pay for the amount of time the lane is used. In most cases, it is a lane charge not a per person charge; thus, up to five bowlers can use a lane and bowl ninety minutes, for example, and split the total time charge five ways. The time rate is usually quoted per half hour or per hour, but the computer keeps track of the number of minutes the lane is on and prorates the charge per minute. Therefore, if you bowl forty-five minutes you pay for forty-five minutes and not a full hour. Some establishments refer to this as renting a lane.

Computerized Score Keeping

Another new trend in bowling is computerized score keeping. In the early days of bowling in the United States, paper and pencil were the major means of recording the individual's or team's score. Figure 11.1 is an example of a very early scoreboard

Figure 11.1
Early paper-and-pencil scoring device.
(Courtesy of National Bowling Hall of Fame and Museum)

Figure 11.2
Computerized scoring display.

device used for league bowling. The device was not conducive to spectator viewing since only the members of the team could see their scores.

More establishments today are converting their houses from the telescore viewing devices to the computerized scoring device shown in figure 11.2. However, computerization is a costly addition and not all establishments are able to make the conversion.

Many amateur tournaments use computerized scorekeeping because obtaining human scorekeepers for an extended period requires much organization and scheduling and is a difficult chore. For several years, the national tournaments of the American Bowling Congress and the Women's International Bowling Congress have used establishments with computerized scoring. In figure 11.3, the very sophisticated computerized scoreboard for the American Bowling Congress National Tournament is shown during the opening ceremony. The bowlers are preparing to begin tournament play.

Computers are able to do an efficient job of scoring, but bowling scores have only a maximum of 300 points per game and require only simple addition and subtraction. From a teaching perspective, it is more desirable for future bowlers to learn how to score and to pass on this valuable and simple skill to our youth. Knowledge of scoring adds to the complete understanding of the traditions of the game and greater enjoyment in participating.

Figure 11.4 shows the entrance to the National Bowling Stadium in Reno, Nevada. This facility with its distinctive geodesic dome contains eighty lanes whose bowling area is as long as 1½ football fields. It opened in 1995 at a cost of 50 million dollars. The American Bowling Congress held their national tournament here in 1996 and the Women's International Bowling Congress tournament is being held at the Stadium in 1997.

Figure 11.3
Computerized scoreboard at ABC National Tournament in Corpus Christi, Texas.

Figure 11.4
Entrance to National Bowling Stadium in Reno, Nevada, 1997.

Figure 11.5
Charlene Agne-Traub prior to WIBC tournament play at the National Bowling Stadium in Reno, Nevada, March 1997.

The lead author of this text is shown in figure 11.5 about to bowl her singles and doubles events at the new National Stadium. She entered the tournament with a 173 average and scored 1,637 in nine games to average 181.9 for the WIBC tournament.

If a local alley uses a time system for bowling fees, take advantage of the opportunity to practice spare pickups. What are the advantages and disadvantages in comparison with payment by game?

Other Ways to Have Fun Bowling

12

The essential skills of bowling and the experience of league bowling are just some of the competitive aspects of the game. The desire to improve your score is compelling whether you are a beginning or an advanced bowler. There are times, however, when the repetition of the activity or competitive event may lead to loss of concentration, boredom, frustration, or perhaps staleness. This is the time to explore the novelty events, such as Scotch Doubles, Pin Point Bowl, and Cocked Hat. Not only are the titles unique but so are the opportunities for continued practice.

Novelty events or variations of regulation bowling are a fun approach to competition and lend themselves to coeducational groupings. They can be used for parties and diversions from regular league play. They are frequently added as a tournament event, and they are excellent for fund-raising endeavors.

Some novelty events are especially suited to beginners or low-average bowlers because of modified scoring and/or cooperation with a partner; others are designed for the advanced bowler. Even though they are variations of regular play, they stress the basic skill components of the game. These events are excellent for sharpening the bowling eye, refining the timing of your delivery, and helping you learn to cope with the pressure involved in performing.

The following games make use of standard equipment and standard lanes. They do not require special devices or score sheets. Some are for the individual bowler; some may be modified to include a partner; and some are specifically designed for doubles.

Variations of Regulation Bowling

Best Ball Doubles

Usually higher scores are rolled in this game than in regulation play, and it affords good practice for spares.

Guidelines for Best Ball

1. Two bowlers are bowling for only one score.
2. Partners are on an adjacent pair of lanes and each one rolls a first ball.
3. The bowler rolling the best ball (the one who knocked down the most pins) sits down.
4. The partner of that bowler comes over to the other lane and tries to pick up the remaining pins to convert the spare or split that has been left.

5. If either partner rolls a strike, this is used as the team's score (since it was the best ball in that frame).
6. If both partners leave the same number of pins, they decide who should pick up the other one's spare.
7. Regular scoring is used.

Scotch Doubles

A partnership game in which partners roll every other ball throughout the line. It is named Scotch (or Dutch) because two bowlers are sharing one game.

Guidelines for Scotch Doubles

1. Each team decides which partner should roll the first ball. (In tournament play, there can be a stipulation that the woman or man must roll the first ball or that the weaker or stronger bowler must do so.)
2. The partner rolls the second ball, and this alternating pattern continues throughout the game.
3. A strike changes the alternating pattern. For example, if the woman is rolling the first ball of each frame and she makes a strike, then the man rolls the first ball in the next frame.
4. Regular scoring is used.

Headpin

An individual game in which the bowler rolls only one ball per frame but scores nothing unless the headpin goes down. This game is scored as in regular bowling (there are no spares) with a perfect game being 120 points.

Guidelines for Headpin Variations

1. The first ball must hit either the 1–3 or 1–2 pocket; if this is achieved, the number of pins knocked down is recorded, and the bowler gets a second ball. If the pocket is not hit (the 1, 2, or 3 pins stand), the first ball is scored as a miss, pins are reset, the second ball is rolled, and any pins knocked down are recorded. If the pocket is missed following a mark, the bonus is lost or reduced. This game will lead to lower scores, especially for beginners, but it does stress control and accuracy on the first ball.
2. A simple scoring for Headpin is a point system whereby the pocket hit on the first ball scores ten points, the pocket contacted on the second ball scores five points, and a pocket missed scores zero.

Least Pins

An interesting and exacting event that demands concentration on those difficult single-spare leaves. It can be used as an individual or partner game.

Now I've got
the roll of things.

♪ ♪ ♪ ♩

Guidelines for Least Pins

1. The object is to knock down the smallest number of pins without rolling the ball into the gutter.
2. The first partner must knock down the 7 or 10 pin, and the second bowler must put his or her ball in exactly the same place.
3. The lowest score (best score) would be "1" for each frame.
4. You may alternate from the 7 to the 10 pin for each frame, or you may have each partner try for one pin. In the latter variation, the lowest score (best score) for ten frames would be 20.
5. Penalties for gutter ball: first ball loss of turn; second ball two points.

Pin Point Bowl

An individual game for intermediate or advanced bowlers.

Guidelines for Pin Point

1. The bowler rolls only one ball in the first and tenth frame but is allowed two balls on frames two through nine.
2. The objective is to get a strike in the first frame and then to knock down one less pin in each succeeding frame. For example, in the second frame, you should knock down nine pins, leaving one, and in the third frame, you should knock down eight pins, leaving two.
3. The scoring is modified so a 300 game can be the final score if each frame is perfect. If the number of pins knocked down in each frame follows the objective (10, 9, 8, 7, 6, 5, 4, 3, 2, 1), the scoring for each frame will be 10, 10, 20, 20, 30, 30, 40, 40, 50, 50 to equal 300.
4. A score of zero is recorded in any frame in which the designated number of pins do not fall.

If you feel that your skills are no match for these novelty events, then the following games may be more fun for you.

No Tap

If you have a good delivery and your ball hits the pocket with some consistency but you still don't strike, you can ease your frustration by playing this game. No Tap

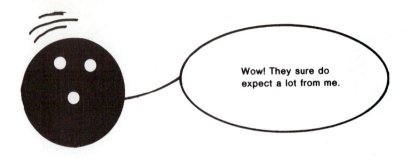

follows all procedures of a regular game except that when the bowler knocks down nine pins on the first ball it is counted as an automatic strike. Many times a roll appears to be a strike but for various reasons one pin remains standing—the definition of a tap. This novelty game makes a tap impossible, and the bowler is awarded a strike on the first ball when nine pins fall.

3–6–9 Tournament

If your score never seems to meet your expectations, treat yourself to a game of 3–6–9. It can be an individual or team event, and it follows regulation rules except that no ball is rolled in the third, sixth, and ninth frames. The bowler is awarded an automatic strike for each of these three frames!

Blind Bowling

This is a perennially popular game that affords excellent practice for spot bowling. A wire string with a curtain (or sheet) is hung above the lane, about halfway down, to block the bowler's view of the pins. Regular scoring is used, and the automatic pinsetter shows the spare setup so the bowler knows at which pins to throw the second ball. Other events can be enjoyed if a pinboy or technician is available.

Cocked Hat

The 3–7–10 pins are set up for right-handers or the 2–7–10 for left-handers. Two balls are rolled each frame, and scoring is similar to regular bowling except strikes and spares score only three instead of ten points.

Cocked Hat and Feather

The 1–3–7–10 pins are set up (or 1–2–7–10), and play is the same as in Cocked Hat. Strikes and spares score four points. A variation of this game can be used with a 1–5–7–10 setup. The objective is to leave the 5 pin standing. If it is upset, there is no score in that frame.

Progressive Splits

A game for the skilled player who wants concentrated split practice. Any split can be chosen, but the setup should start with the easiest splits, such as the 2–7, 3–10, 4–5, and then progress to the most difficult, such as the 4–10, 6–7–10, and 4–7–10. Avoid the impossible splits.

You may be familiar with some of these events, and you may have used a different set of rules from those outlined. These games are not a part of official league bowling, so they may be played in various ways.

Practice

Practice is the extra element that leads to success in bowling. There is no substitute for it. Although mental preparation and strategy are beneficial, the refinement of a good approach and the consistency of a well-timed delivery are essential. This refinement and consistency can be developed through individual practice, league bowling, or use of novelty events in bowling.

This book has attempted to give you a point of reference or a basis for building good bowling habits. Each bowler will develop his or her own style, methods for practice, and best working pace. Discover it, stay with it, and enjoy a fascinating game in the process.

The Language of Bowling

13

Bowler's Lingo

Almost every sport has a language all its own, and bowling can claim what is probably one of the most colorful vocabularies. The terminology may vary from place to place, however. Bowlers in Los Angeles and Chicago call a 1–2 pocket hit for right-handers a "Brooklyn," whereas the Brooklynites call it a "Jersey." Most of the terminology listed here is widely used, but space is left for you to insert other lingo peculiar to your locale.

Remember that to master all aspects of bowling you should "talk" a good game as well as demonstrate it.

Terms Relating to the Ball

Bridge
Distance between finger holes on the ball.

Brooklyn
Ball hitting to the left of the headpin (1–2 pocket) for right-handed bowlers.

Creeper
A very slow ball.

Crossover
Same as "Brooklyn."

Curve
A ball that has a wide sweeping arc, a wider bend than a hook.

Dead ball
A poorly rolled ball that deflects off course.

Flat apple or flat ball
Same as "dead ball."

Gutter ball
A poorly rolled ball that goes off the lane into the gutter (channel) before reaching the pins.

Hook
A ball that travels straight down the lane for a distance, then breaks sharply to the pocket as it nears the pins.

Loft
Throwing the ball too far out on the lane beyond the foul line so that it travels in the air ten inches or more before hitting the lane.

Pitch
The angle at which the thumb and/or fingerholes are bored in the ball.

Reverse hook
A ball that breaks to the right for a right-handed bowler.

Span
Distance between thumb and finger holes on the ball.

Working ball
A hook ball effective in producing a great deal of pin action through drive power.

. . . .

Terms Relating to the Bowler

ABBA
The American Blind Bowling Association; the sanctioning and guiding organization for blind bowlers.

ABC
American Bowling Congress; official rules-making body of tenpin bowling for men and mixed competition.

AJBC
American Junior Bowling Congress, since replaced by YABA.

Anchor
A person bowling in last position on a team, usually the one with the highest average.

Choke
To fail to convert a spare or strike under pressure.

FIQ
Federation Internationale des Quilleurs; the world governing body for bowling for men and women. It divides its world into three geographical zones: American, Asian, and European.

Foul
When a part of the bowler's person touches or goes beyond the foul line as the ball is delivered; usually indicated by a buzzer or a light when the line is touched.

Kegler
Another name for bowler coming from the German word *kegel*.

Scratch bowler
A bowler who has no handicap—has topnotch average.

USTBF
United States Tenpin Bowling Federation; recognized by the IOC, USOC, and FIQ as the national governing body for national and international amateur bowling competition in the United States.

WIBC
Women's International Bowling Congress, 1925 to present.

WNBA
Women's National Bowling Association, November 18, 1916–1925, was replaced by the WIBC.

YABA

Young American Bowling Alliance; rule-making body for youth tenpin bowling.

. . . .

General Terms Relating to the Lanes

Alley

Another name for lane; term more commonly used prior to the 1960s. Also the section of pine and maple from the foul line to the pit on which the ball is rolled.

Approach

The fifteen-foot-long maple section of the lane that the bowler walks on while delivering the ball before reaching the foul line. Also, the three, four, or five steps taken in preparation for delivery of the ball.

Arrow

Aiming checkpoints embedded in the lanes and used as directional guides.

Channel

A modern term for the gutter.

Foul line

The line that separates the approach from the lane.

Graveyard

The lane or lanes that are toughest for a bowler to score on.

Guide rail

A guide for blind bowlers positioned on the approach.

Gutter

Either side or deep groove of alley bed that catches misdirected balls or errant pins (See Channel).

Kickbacks

The division or side boards at the pit end of the lane.

Locator dots (spots)

Dots positioned seven feet beyond the foul line and used by spot bowlers as a target.

Pit

The space at the end of the lane where the pins fall when hit by the ball.

Return

The track on which the ball rolls back from the pit to the ball rack.

Spot (range finder or arrow)

A certain place on the lane either seven feet or sixteen feet beyond the line at which the bowler aims.

Lane Conditions

Holding

A fast lane that cuts down on the amount of hook.

Rough, tough, or mean

Lanes that are difficult to score on.

Running

A slow lane that allows more hook.

Soft
Lanes that are easy to score on.

Stiff
Same as fast or holding lane.

. . . .

Terms Relating to the Pins

Baby split
The 2–7 or 3–10 splits.

Bedposts
The 7–10 split.

Big four
The 4–6–7–10 split; also known as "double pinochle."

Bucket
The 2–4–5–8 leave or 3–5–6–9 leave.

Cherry
Picking off the front pin of a spare and leaving other pins standing; also referred to as a chop. *Example:* the 5 and 9 pins, hit the 5 pin and leave the 9 pin.

Chop
(See Cherry).

Dead wood
Fallen pins left lying on the lane or gutter after the ball has been rolled.

Headpin
The number 1 pin.

Kingpin
The number 5 pin.

Leave
The pins remaining after the first ball is rolled in a frame.

Pocket or "strike zone"
The space between the 1 and 3 pins for a right-handed bowler, or the 1 and 2 pins for a left-handed bowler.

Railroad
Synonym for split.

Sleeper
A pin hidden, or obscured from easy view, directly behind another pin; sometimes called "double wood."

Split
Two or more pins left standing after the first delivery, provided the headpin (1 pin) is down and (a) at least one pin is down between two or more standing pins (e.g., 7 and 9, 2 and 7 pins), or (b) at least one pin is down immediately ahead of two or more standing pins (e.g., 5 and 6 pins).

Tap
Leaving just one pin, either the 4 or 7 or 8 or 10 pin, on what appeared to be a strike ball.

Washout

The 1–2–4–10 leave for a right-hander; the 1–3–6–7 leave for a left-hander.

. . . .

Terms Relating to Scoring

Average

An indication of a bowler's ability and computed by dividing the total number of pins knocked down by the total number of games rolled.

Blind

Score given a team for an absent member; either ten pins less their average or a score of 120. Sometimes called absentee score.

Blow

An error; failure to spare (except following a split).

Double

Two strikes in succession during a game.

Dutch 200 or Dutchman

A 200 game consisting of alternating strikes and spares.

Frame

The box on the score sheet in which the score is registered; one-tenth of a game (aside from game-end bonuses).

Handicap

A method of scoring that enables individuals or teams with different averages to compete against one another by adding pins to the lower-average person or to the team score.

Line

A game of ten frames.

Mark

Getting a strike or spare.

Miss

Failure to mark; same as a blow. Splits are also misses but are excusable in the bowler's mind.

Open frame

A frame without a strike or spare.

Perfect game

A game of 300 achieved by rolling twelve strikes in a row. On February 12, 1930, in Madison, Wisconsin, Jennie Hoverson's 300 was the first perfect game in the history of the WIBC (fig. 13.1).

Scratch

Using actual scores without handicaps.

Spare

All pins knocked down on two balls.

Steal

To get more pins than you shoot for.

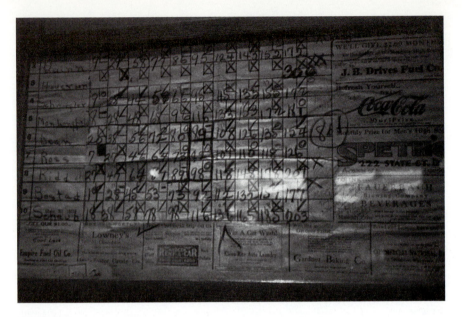

Figure 13.1
Perfect game—300 score. (Courtesy of National Bowling Hall of Fame and Museum)

Strike
All pins knocked down on the first ball.

Strike out
Three successive strikes in the tenth frame, or striking to finish the game.

Turkey
Three strikes in a row during a game.

Vacancy
A score to be used when a member is absent and a substitute is not obtained. The vacancy score is usually 120 unless otherwise specified by league rules.

. . . .

Define the terms Brooklyn, sleeper, cherry, scratch, and turkey.

References

Allen, George. *The Mental Game: The Inner Game of Bowling.* Deerfield, Ill.: Tech-Ed, 1983.

Allen, George, and Dick Ritger. *The Complete Guide to Bowling Spares.* Deerfield, Ill.: Tech-Ed, 1986.

American Bowling Congress. *Playing Rules, 1995–1996.* Greendale, Wis.: ABC/WIBC (Published annually.)

Aulby, Mike, and Dave Ferraro with Dan Herbst. *Bowling 200+.* Chicago, Ill.: Contemporary Books, 1990.

Baker, William. *Sports in the Western World.* Rev. ed. Urbana and Chicago, Ill.: University of Illinois Press, 1988.

Grinfelds, Velma. *Right Down Your Alley: The Complete Book of Bowling.* 3d ed. Englewood, Colo.: Morton Activity Series, 1992.

Kouros, Thomas C. *PAR Bowling.* Palatine, Ill.: Progressive Bowling Development, 1976.

Luby, Mort. "The History of Bowling." *Bowlers Journal* 70, no. 11 (November 1983): 5–171.

Mackey, Richard T. *Bowling.* Palo Alto, Calif.: National Press Books, 1974.

McWhirter, Norris, and Ross McWhirter. *Guinness Book of World Records.* N.Y.: Bantam Books, 1977.

National Association for Girls and Women in Sport. *Bowling-Fencing Guide.* Washington, D.C.: American Alliance for Health, Physical Education and Recreation. (Published at even-year intervals.)

National Bowling Council. *The Bowling Instructor's Handbook.* Washington, D.C.: NBC's Education Service Center, 1974.

National Bowling Council. *Instructor's Manual Learn to Bowl Plus.* Washington, D.C.: NBC's Education Service Center, 1976.

Pezzano, Chuck. *Professional Bowlers Association Guide to Better Bowling.* N.Y.: Simon and Schuster, 1974.

Porter, David, ed. *Biographical Dictionary of American Sports, 1992–95 Supplement for Baseball, Football, Basketball and Other Sports.* Westport, Conn.: Greenwood Press, 1995.

Ritger, Dick, and Judy Soutar. *Bowlers Guide.* Greendale, Wis.: ABC-WIBC. 1976.

Scott, Thomas, and Carol Carpenter. *Bowling Everyone.* Winston-Salem, N.C.: Hunter Textbooks, 1985.

Strickland, Robert. *Bowling: Steps to Success.* Champaign, Ill.: Leisure Press, 1989.

Taylor, Bill. *Fitting and Drilling a Bowling Ball.* San Gabriel, Calif.: BT Products, 1984.

Weber, Dick. *Weber on Bowling.* San Jose, Calif.: Stone Walled Press, 1987.

Women's International Bowling Congress. *Playing Rules and Bylaws, 1991–1992.* Greendale, Wis.: WIBC. (Published annually.)

National Bowling Periodicals

Bowling Digest. 900 Grove St., Evanston, IL 60201. Phone: 312–491–6440.

Bowl Magazine. Official Publication of the Nation's Capital Area Bowling Association, 4710 Auth Place, Suite 465 Camp Springs, MD, 20746–4202. Phone: 301–899–5979.

Bowlers Journal. National Bowlers Journal, Inc., Suite 1801, John Hancock Center, 875 No. Michigan Ave., Chicago, IL 60611. Phone: 312–266–7171.

The Bowling Proprietor. 375 West Higgins Rd., Hoffman Estates, IL 60172.

The Woman Bowler. WIBC, 5301 S. 76th St., Greendale, WI 53129–1127.

Young American Bowling Alliance World. 5301 S. 76th St., Greendale, WI 53129–1127.

Films or Videos and Film or Video Distributors

Learn to Bowl Series (National Bowling Council). 1976. Sound Slidefilm Richard Manufacturing Company, Van Nuys, Calif.
"Let It Happen"
"Watch It Happen"
"Put It All Together"
"Strikes and Spares"
"Personal Adjustments"
"Playing Lanes"
"The Release"
"Building on Fundamentals"
"Think It Through"
"Learn to Bowl, Plus" (advanced)
"Learn to Bowl" (Program for Youth)
Summit Media Co.
P.O. Box 55184
Valencia, CA 91385
Phone: 1–800–777–8668

Videos:
Johnson, Don. "Pro's Guide to Better Bowling," Vols. 1 and 2.
Burton, Nelson. "Bo." "Score More by Bowling."
Cambridge Physical Education & Health.
One Players club Dr., Dept. PE2, Charleston, WV 25311
Phone: 1–800–468–4227
Videos:
"Bowling with Lisa Wagner and Wayne Webb" (SK 900 V).
Earl Anthony, "Bowl to Win" (MXS 700 V).
Earl Anthony, "Going for 300" (MXS 710 V).

Bowling Directory—Associations and Facilities

American Blind Bowling Association
411 Sheriff St.
Mercer, PA 16137
Phone: 412–662–5748

American Bowling Congress
5301 S. 76th St.
Greendale, WI 53129–1127
Phone: 414–421–6400
FAX: 414–421–1194

American Wheelchair Bowling Association
5809 NE 21st Ave.
Ft. Lauderdale, FL 33308
Phone: 916–243–2695
FAX: 916–243–2695

Bowling Hall of Fame and Museum
111 Stadium Plaza
St. Louis, MO 63102
Phone: 314–231–6340
FAX: 314–231–4054

National Bowling Stadium
P. O. Box 837

Reno, NV 89504
Phone: 1–800–304–BOWL

National Deaf Bowling Association
2208 Gateway Oakes Dr. #192
Sacramento, CA 95833
Phone: 916–564–8328
RELAY: 800–735–2922

National Duckpin Bowling Congress
Linthicum, MD 21090
Phone: 410–636–2695
FAX: 410–636–3256

Woman's International Bowling Congress
5301 S. 76th St.
Greendale, WI 53129–1191
Phone: 414–421–9000
FAX: 414–421–3013

Young American Bowling Alliance
5301 S. 76th St.
Greendale, WI 53129–1192
Phone: 414–421–4700
FAX: 414–421–1301

Questions and Answers

General Instructions: Answer questions from the perspective of a right-handed bowler.

True or False

1. A line consists of ten frames. (p. 61)
2. A strike in the tenth frame entitles the bowler to two more balls. (p. 62)
3. A frame consists of bowling two balls. (p. 109)
4. A split is recorded thus: $\boxed{0}$ (p. 61)
5. The recommended point of aim is the 1–3 pocket. (p. 38)
6. If bowlers on adjoining lanes are ready to start their approaches at the same time, the bowler on the left is given the courtesy of bowling first. (p. 69)
7. On a four-step delivery, the first three steps should be longer than the fourth. (p. 29)
8. The Brooklyn pocket is the 1–2 pocket. (p. 105)
9. Crossing the foul line when bowling voids any score you receive in that frame. (p. 61)
10. A spare is recorded with an: $\boxed{X}$ (p. 61)
11. To pick up the 7 pin, a bowler should move the starting position slightly right and the point of aim to the left. (pp. 45–46)
12. Pulling the arm across the body after releasing the ball is called "side-wheeling." (p. 56)
13. A ball breaking to the right down the alley is a "hook" ball. (p. 25)
14. As a general rule, roll spares at cross angles. (p. 43)
15. To pick up the 2, 4, and 8 pins, roll the ball from the left side of the alley. (p. 46)
16. The spot aiming technique is best for bowlers using a straight ball; the pin technique is used most by bowlers using a hook or curve. (p. 38)
17. The position of the hand for the hook delivery is "thumb at ten o'clock, fingers at four o'clock." (p. 25)
18. In the four-step delivery, the ball is pushed away from the body on the second step. (p. 27)
19. Pins knocked down by another pin rebounding in play from the side partition or rear cushion are counted as pins down. (p. 65)

20. Most experts use the pins as their point of aim because they are seen more easily than the spot. (p. 38)
21. A spare is marked with a horizontal dash (—) in the appropriate box. (p. 61)
22. After the release, a bowler should lean away from the foul line and balance by stepping on the right foot. (p. 31)
23. To pick up the 6 and 10 pins, a bowler releases the ball from the right side of the alley. (pp. 45–46)
24. To knock down the 1, 3, and 5 pins, roll from the right side of the alley. (p. 42)
25. Pins knocked down by a ball that leaves the alley prior to hitting the pins shall not count. (p. 66)
26. A foul is charged against a player if he steps over the foul detecting device to avoid fouling. (p. 65)
27. Between balls, a bowler should step to the rear of the approach. (p. 69)
28. An error is recorded as a diagonal line when scoring: ▱ (p. 61)
29. The release spot at the foul line is the point of aim for the spot bowler. (pp. 38–39)
30. In using a four-step approach, a bowler starts with the right foot. (p. 27)
31. Lanes that have just been cleaned and oiled are usually fast and cut down the amount of hook on the ball. (p. 79)
32. A bowler's primary objective is to develop maximum speed of the ball in order to attain the highest pin count. (p. 17)
33. Regulation bowling balls range in weight from 10 to 20 pounds. (p. 73)
34. In the conventional grip, the fingers and thumb are inserted in the holes to the first joint. (p. 19)
35. In most situations after a split occurs, the average bowler should "play it safe" and attempt to get one pin of two, or two of three or four. (p. 87)
36. The Dutch are responsible for introducing bowling in America in 1626. (p. 2)
37. Since its early development in this country, bowling has always been considered a clean and wholesome activity for American youth. (p. 4)
38. Most beginners should learn to bowl with a 15- or 16-pound ball. (p. 73)
39. A bowler with a great amount of hook should select a point of aim more to the right of the second arrow. (p. 38)
40. A reverse hook style of delivery is recommended for left-handed bowlers. (p. 50)
41. In spare bowling, if all else is forgotten, plan on hitting the pin closest to you to get your spare. (p. 43)
42. When lifting a ball from the rack or turntable, the ball should be lifted with both hands placed on the sides of the ball, away from other oncoming balls. (p. 19)
43. In delivering a hook ball, a bowler should feel the thumb release first, then the fingers. (p. 29)

44. The letters ABC refer to the national bowling organization called the Allied Bowling Council. (p. 106)
45. To remedy a ball hitting squarely on the headpin, the bowler can move his or her starting position slightly to the left. (p. 40)
46. A bowler can increase the velocity of the ball by holding it higher— at chest or chin level in the starting position. (p. 22)
47. The release point at the foul line should be in the vicinity of the center dot. (p. 40)
48. In learning to develop the proper sense of timing in the four-step approach, a bowler should practice the step pattern first, then fit the arm swing pattern to the step pattern. (p. 25)
49. Taps are usually the result of poor ball action. (p. 48)
50. A split occurs when a bowler's first ball hits too "high" on the headpin. (p. 108)
51. When a bowler bowls out of turn, the pins knocked down do not count, but the bowler is allowed to rebowl. (pp. 66–67)
52. Dead wood refers to pins that are cracked or damaged. (p. 108)
53. Pitch is the degree of inclination the finger and thumbholes have toward the center of the ball. (p. 75)
54. Bowling shoes are a necessity for efficient performance because the right shoe has a leather tip, rubber sole, and heel; whereas, the left shoe has a smooth leather sole. (p. 76)
55. When a system of marking is used in handicap bowling, each mark represents ten pins. (p. 85)
56. The hook on the ball is accomplished by applying force off center. (pp. 31–33)
57. For the proper starting position in the four-step approach, most of the body weight is on the right foot to act as a reminder that the first step should be taken on the left foot. (pp. 23–24)
58. The straight ball delivery requires less hand and wrist strength than the hook ball delivery. (p. 31)
59. The term *straight ball* refers to the direction the ball takes; it should be rolled down the middle of the alley. (p. 31)
60. The finger holes for the "straight" ball should be at approximately six o'clock. (p. 32)
61. In checking a well-balanced follow-through position at the foul line, the toe and knee of the left leg should form a vertical line with the shoulder. (pp. 30–31)
62. To add more hook, there should be more turnover of the right hand at release. (p. 30)
63. On a perfect hit, the ball contacts only four pins. (p. 42)
64. Most expert bowlers spot bowl the first ball and pin bowl the second ball. (p. 39)
65. A bowler rolling consistently right of the spot is likely to be releasing the ball too soon, before the fourth step is completed. (p. 58)

Score Totals

Instructions for 66–75: Complete the frames by placing the correct score in the boxes.

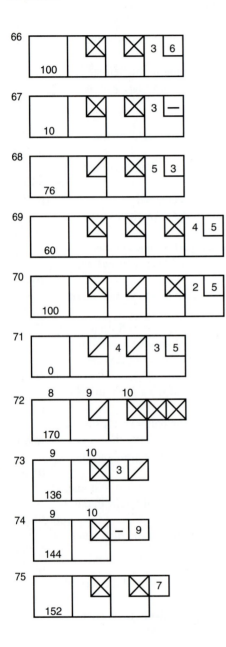

Matching

76. railroad (p. 87)
77. error (p. 55)
78. middle spare (p. 44)
79. Brooklyn hit (p. 46)
80. left-side spare (p. 45)
81. to equalize teams (p. 82)
82. lane (p. 3)
83. bedposts (p. 108)
84. hook ball (p. 25)
85. sleeper (p. 44)
86. bucket (p. 108)
87. baby split (p. 108)
88. a frame without a strike or spare (p. 62)
89. chopping off front pin (p. 44)
90. spot bowling (p. 38)
91. releasing ball noisily beyond foul line (p. 57)
92. straight ball (p. 32)
93. term for "bowler" (p. 1)
94. three strikes in a row (p. 63)
95. right-side spare (p. 46)
96. distance between finger holes (p. 20)
97. the number 5 pin (p. 41)
98. strike or spare (p. 61)
99. using actual scores in competition (p. 109)
100. two strikes in a row (p. 63)

1. 7–10 split
2. thumb at 12 o'clock
3. *Kegler*
4. 3–6–10
5. cherry
6. open
7. bubble
8. lemon
9. 2–4–5–8
10. range finder
11. scratch
12. a hidden pin
13. 5–9
14. turkey
15. blow
16. split
17. 4–7–8
18. loft
19. curling
20. eagle
21. chicken
22. 1–2 pocket
23. 2–7
24. kingpin
25. double
26. lob
27. thumb at 7 o'clock
28. bridge
29. alley
30. mark
31. thumb at 10 o'clock
32. handicap

Knowledge Test Answer Key

True or False

1. T	14. T	27. T	40. F	53. T
2. T	15. F	28. F	41. T	54. T
3. F	16. F	29. F	42. T	55. T
4. T	17. T	30. T	43. T	56. T
5. F	18. F	31. T	44. F	57. F
6. F	19. T	32. F	45. T	58. T
7. F	20. F	33. F	46. T	59. F
8. T	21. F	34. F	47. F	60. T
9. F	22. F	35. T	48. F	61. T
10. F	23. F	36. T	49. F	62. F
11. T	24. T	37. F	50. T	63. T
12. F	25. T	38. F	51. T	64. F
13. F	26. T	39. T	52. F	65. F

Score Totals

66. 151	68. 122	70. 164	72. 220	74. 163
67. 49	69. 142	71. 35	73. 156	75. 196

Matching

76. (16)	81. (32)	86. (9)	91. (18)	96. (28)
77. (15)	82. (29)	87. (23)	92. (2)	97. (24)
78. (13)	83. (1)	88. (6)	93. (3)	98. (30)
79. (22)	84. (31)	89. (5)	94. (14)	99. (11)
80. (17)	85. (12)	90. (10)	95. (4)	100. (25)

Index